Teaching
Film
at GCSE

James Baker and Patrick Toland

Series Editor: Vivienne Clark
Commissioning Editor: Wendy Earle

British Library Cataloguing-in-Publication Data
A catalogue record for this guide is available from the British Library

ISBN 9781844571512

First published in 2007 by the British Film Institute
21 Stephen Street, London W1T 1LN

Student worksheets to support this guide are supplied at: <www.bfi.org.uk/tms>
User name: **filmgcse@bfi.org.uk** Password: **gc1603fi**

Design: Amanda Hawkes
Cover photograph: Toby Maguire in *Spider-Man* (Sam Raimi, 2002) courtesy of BFI Stills
Printed in Great Britain by Cromwell Press Ltd

www.bfi.org.uk

There's more to discover about film and television through the BFI. Our world-renowned archive, cinemas, festivals, films, publications and learning resources are here to inspire you.

Introduction to the series

Moving image media play a central role in the lives of young people as a major source of information and entertainment, and a major influence on their ideas about the world. Only gradually has this been recognised in school curricula, and over the past decade there has been a rapid increase in the number of students opting to take Media Studies at GCSE, while increasingly there is a recognition of moving image media in English at GCSE, as represented – in particular – by the new Edexcel English Studies GCSE. In addition, it appears that there are plans to commence Film Studies at GCSE level in 2009 to introduce this specialist focus of study to younger students and to provide opportunities for progression for the highly successful A level Film Studies.

Unfortunately many teachers are thrown in at the deep end to teach the subject. There are very few teacher-training courses in this country devoted to Film or Media studies. Coming from backgrounds in other subjects, teachers may have little specific knowledge of the way moving image media create meaning. In addition, the institutional context of why and how films and television programmes are made may be a mystery to them, and the practical aspects of actually making films – even with the (relatively) cheap to buy, easy-to-use new technologies – may seem rather daunting. So this series is aimed, first and foremost, at those teachers. It offers a down-to-earth introduction to teaching about film (book 1), digital video production (book 2), and television (book 3), and broadly follows the same format that we used for the highly successful *Teaching Film and Media Studies* A Level series that we launched in 2002.

Moreover, even teachers with some experience of teaching GCSE Media Studies may find their practice refreshed by using these books, packed as they are with information and suggestions from experienced teachers of the subject. Likewise, experienced teachers of GCSE English will find many rich resources here for the teaching of media texts relevant to their own specification contexts, together with invaluable guidance on best practice and accessible suggestions for ways of tackling challenging topics and methods of teaching and learning, such as those associated with hands-on media production with GCSE level students.

Each book is supported by schemes of work for Media Studies and English, as well as online worksheets which can be downloaded, printed and used with students.

This first guide in the series introduces film – a rich and varied medium – which can provide stunning insights to other worlds – real and imaginary. The authors have a great deal of experience in introducing students to this subject, inspiring them to interrogate a wide range of films, how they are produced and how they make meaning. We hope that any teacher will find much of value here, and will use this book as a key resource to extend the range of materials used and enhance teaching practice.

Vivienne Clark
Series Editor

Wendy Earle
Comissioning Editor

About the authors

James Baker

James Baker is Head of Media Studies at Hurtwood House School in Surrey. He is the author of several media textbooks, a freelance writer and teacher trainer in media education and a senior examiner for a major examining board.

Patrick Toland

Patrick Toland is an experienced teacher of Media Studies, English and Philosophy at Hurtwood House School and a freelance writer.

Series editor

Vivienne Clark is a teacher of Film and Media Studies at Langley Park School for Boys, Beckenham, Kent and an Advanced Skills Teacher. She is currently an Associate Tutor of bfi Education and formerly a Principal Examiner for A Level Media Studies for one of the English awarding bodies. She is also a freelance teacher trainer, media education consultant and writer/editor, with several published textbooks and resources, including *GCSE Media Studies* (Longman 2002), *Key Concepts and Skills for Media Studies* (Hodder Arnold 2002) and *The Complete A-Z Film and Media Studies Handbook* (Hodder and Stoughton 2007).

Introduction

It is one of the ironies of education that, while almost every teacher in every subject has at some point used film or video as a teaching aid, there is still little agreement as to the validity of teaching about the moving image in its own right. Those most in favour of some systematic attempt to teach students about the language and significance of films are likely to reside in humanities departments, particularly teachers of Media Studies and English. However, even within these areas, film can be regarded with some trepidation at Key Stage 3 and Key Stage 4 and other forms of image analysis, generally print-based, tend to take precedence. To varying degrees in every other department, film study will be regarded with suspicion, or possibly downright hostility.

Despite this academic ambivalence, there has been a clear trend in recent years towards recognising the importance of visual literacy in young learners. The fast-growing uptake of Media and Film Studies at all levels, along with the integration of Media elements in most of the GCSE English specifications, indicate a burgeoning consensus that students need to be given the necessary tools to make sense of the audiovisual texts which saturate their lives. In this relatively youthful field of study, film analysis remains a key skill for students. The ubiquity of film culture across a number of media, its significance to the cultural background of most of our students and the dynamic tension that persists between art and entertainment make the teaching and learning of analytical practice in film of central importance to the modern classroom.

The ability to understand film language is the starting point of proficient visual literacy across a range of media. The influence of film is evident not just on its closest offspring, television, but on advertising, music video, games and other moving image media. Arguably these forms are now as pervasive as the written word in building the fabric of our cultural lives and we need to ensure that students are suitably literate not only in written language but also in that of image and sound.

Understanding film language is only the first step of this educational journey. While film is arguably the most influential medium of the 20th century, its purpose goes beyond simple communication. Film is not just information, but entertainment; not just language, but art. Any study of film (just as the study of a novel or poem) will invoke issues of value that can be addressed with students. Questions about what makes films 'good' or 'bad' are a legitimate part of this

Introduction

debate. While it may be true that the extremes of educational debate have polarised behind the barricades of teacher as moral arbiter or teacher as liberal enabler, most of us acknowledge that we have a responsibility to open our students' minds to debates about value, even if we are going to allow them to form their own judgments. This guide is not produced from the naive perspective that all films are equally worthy of study. Rather we have tried to focus on examples which have worked successfully in our own classes and which we know allow students to explore key issues of film culture. We also have attempted to ensure that the range of films referenced encompasses the kinds of texts which are recognised as commercial products, as well as Hollywood 'classics', alternative and independent films and films from other cultures.

Of course, in the modern classroom the notion of an indigenous culture from which to judge 'others' may well be something of an anachronism already. The multicultural backgrounds of many of our teaching groups adds resonance to the teaching of film, furnishing fascinating comparisons between different cultures and their manifestation in film and related media. In Part 2 we look at some of the issues raised by the idea of film as cultural heritage and examine how particular film texts seem to engage with the notion of national identities. This area of film study is of particular relevance for a 21st-century audience, for whom many of the traditional cultural barriers of film consumption have been removed. DVD, distribution by download and multichannel television all allow British audiences to watch and enjoy films from a variety of cultures. The impact on audiences (and filmmakers) experiencing this bricolage of film styles is still far from obvious in terms of its long-term effects on film languages. Pessimists argue that this kind of globalisation of film culture will lead to the homogenisation of national cinemas, likely to be swamped by the ubiquity of US product. On the other hand, there is evidence that even Hollywood films are not immune (in fact never have been) from the influence of other film cultures – witness the influx of narratives, visual styles and even personnel from Asian cinemas in the last decade or so. We would like to believe that the clear shift in recent Hollywood culture away from the dominance of the high-concept blockbuster to a more varied menu of films, many from a blossoming independent sector, is only one of the results of the emergence of sophisticated and literate film audiences, no longer held hostage by the multiplex. If, as teachers, we can play a small part in the process of helping to build these audiences from our students, then we should be optimistic that film still has a promising future in our digital age.

Teaching Film at GCSE has been written for those teachers who are involved – whether newly or for many years, whether in a small way or for many hours, whether part of a Media Studies, English or other curriculum – in delivering moving image education to their students. It is based upon some key principles: that audiovisual literacy is as important as print literacy; that studying film is worthwhile in its own right; and that understanding film means understanding not only the products, but those who produce and those who consume. However, it has been written with the practicalities of the busy classroom environment in mind. We hope that the guide will go a little way towards defining a workable agenda for film study and thus indicate the growing value of the subject in today's educational arena. However, first and foremost, we hope that it is a valuable tool for the teacher, a road map for what can be a daunting journey into the world of film.

In Part 1, we look at different approaches to teaching film in the classroom, along with some successful strategies for integrating film and learning and some tried and tested schemes of work to be employed or adapted as appropriate. In Part 2, we provide some background for film study by looking at the key concepts, the critical and academic perspectives which have been influential and the historical and industrial contexts which inform both the production of and our consumption of film. In Part 3, we have provided a series of case studies to be used by teachers in a variety of areas. Through comparative studies of specific films within particular genres, we want not only to provide specific material for the classroom but also to show how personal knowledge and examples can help to create an effective learning experience for students.

Assessment contexts

The teaching of film plays a significant role in all of the GCSE specifications for Media Studies. The following table indicates some specific elements which can be met by the study of various aspects of film culture.

Awarding body	Subject	Unit code	Module/Topic
AQA GCSE	Media Studies	3571	Coursework – Section A assignments
OCR GCSE	Media Studies	1918	Components 1/2: Textual Analysis (moving image)
OCR GCSE	Media Studies	1918	Component 7: Coursework
WJEC GCSE	Media Studies		Written Paper – Section A
WJEC GCSE	Media Studies		Coursework: Textual Analysis

All of the specifications emphasise the importance of understanding film in terms of its specific languages, forms and conventions, its audiences and its historical and institutional contexts. The guide has sections on each of these areas and the case studies are also based around these key concepts. In addition, students' understanding of film will inform their own creative and practical work and provide some valuable contextual information for production logs and diaries.

The importance of media literacy is also acknowledged by the inclusion of elements of Media Studies in various English GCSE specifications. Some of the work on the ability to read and analyse media texts is focused on print media, but the following units demand specific engagement with film texts as coursework assignments.

Student worksheets to support this guide are supplied at: **www.bfi.org.uk/tms**

Awarding body	Subject	Unit code	Module/Topic
AQA GCSE	English A	3702	Coursework – Reading and Writing Responses to Media (En3)
Edexcel GCSE	English B	1204	Paper 1B – Unit 2: Response to Media Texts

It is also evident that a great deal of teaching in English and English Literature classes can be informed and aided by film study. In English, the teaching of narrative, characterisation and other structural elements of reading and writing can be helpfully focused by reference to film. The specific study of prose and drama texts in English Literature is often accompanied by film versions, allowing discussion of the creative choices made by filmmakers to inform understanding of the thematic and symbolic elements of a particular novel or play. A typical coursework assignment based on a play by Shakespeare, for example, might ask students to reflect on a film version of that play in relation to staged versions seen or the text as read.

The study of film can be a useful and accessible tool in a variety of other subjects, with film texts providing stimulus for debate and curriculum content. It can also be a vital element in the delivery of Citizenship or PHSE programmes where an understanding of the messages and values of well-chosen examples can be the starting point for a variety of issue-based topics.

Schemes of work

Introduction to film language (see pp26–31)

Week 1

Basic image analysis – still images

Signs and signifiers – content and form

Analysis of image-based print ads – denotations and connotations

Exercise: Use image analysis to show how the product is represented to a target audience – students to present their readings to the class.

Exercise: Ask students to produce their own adverts, selling a product via a relevant visual image.

Week 2

Introduction to *mise en scène*

Importance of setting/location

Character construction – costume and make-up

Lighting, production design, colour

Exercise: Commutation task – change key elements of famous sequences to show how the meanings would change.

Exercise: Analysis of key-sequence examples – eg opening sequence of *Boyz N The Hood* (John Singleton, US, 1991); sequence from *Bullet Boy* (Saul Dibb, UK, 2004).

Week 3

Introduction to camerawork

Shot types and meanings; shot angles and meanings; camera movement and meanings (*Worksheet 6*)

Composition – rule of thirds; deep and shallow focus

Exercise: Analysis of key-sequence examples – eg opening sequence of *The Matrix* (Andy and Larry Wachowski, US/Australia, 1999); sequence from *The Day After Tomorrow* (Roland Emmerich, US, 2004).

Exercise: Ask students to film a six-shot sequence of a mundane task (playing chess, walking and sitting) to demonstrate variety of shot.

Week 4

Introduction to editing

Transitions – cut, dissolve, fade, wipes; montage and meaning

Creating pace through editing – manipulation of time

Student worksheets to support this guide are supplied at: **www.bfi.org.uk/tms**

Creating perspective through editing – narrative information

Exercise: Analysis of key-sequence examples – eg opening sequence of *GoldenEye* (Martin Campbell, UK/US, 1995); sequence from *The Lord of the Rings* (Peter Jackson, US/NZ, 2001).

Exercise: Using *iMovie* or *Windows Movie Editor*, ask students to recut the six shots from Week 3 to change the mood of the sequence.

Week 5

Introduction to sound

Diegetic and non-diegetic sound

Soundtrack and score; incidental music, themes, strings

Ambient sound and sound effects – Foley artists, sound mixing

Exercise: Analysis of key sequence examples eg sequence from *Donnie Darko* (Richard Kelly, US, 2001); sequence from *Mean Girls* (Mark S Waters, US, 2004).

Exercise: Play the soundtrack from a variety of film sequences and ask students to deduce setting, character and narrative from sound alone; compare with complete sequence.

Exercise: Ask students to add a library soundtrack to their edited sequence to establish a desired atmosphere.

Week 6

Introduction to visual and special effects

CGI; prosthetics; pyrotechnics; ballistics

Exercise: Analysis of key-sequence examples eg sequence from *Spider-Man* (Sam Raimi, US, 2002); sequence from *Superman Returns* (Bryan Singer, US, 2006).

Exercise: Ask students to write analyses of film sequences – structure, terminology, argument.

Adapting Shakespeare for the screen
(see pp113–121)

Week 1

Introduction to Shakespearean adaptations

Focus on differences between theatrical and cinematic portrayals

Exercise: Examine adaptations of Shakespeare from the 1940s and 50s and discuss their content and tone (see

<www.screenonline.org.uk>). Ask students to judge them against stage versions. What recommends cinema?

Invite an actor (preferably with film experience) from a theatre company that performs Shakespeare plays (eg The RSC education department) to visit and be interviewed by students.

Week 2

The modern renaissance of Shakespeare adaptations

The abridging and translation of texts – how *mise en scène* serves to replicate and reinvent the original play

Exercise: Get students to create their own *mise en scène* sketches and proposals for any Shakespeare play or perhaps select one and see how individual students produce different 'visions' in the same way that filmmakers do.

Exercise: Analysis of key-sequence examples – *William Shakespeare's Romeo + Juliet* (Baz Luhrmann, US/Canada, 1996)

Exercise: This version of *Romeo and Juliet* has been praised/criticised for its MTV/music video style. Contrast it with a music video with a similar soundtrack and a musical version of the play *West Side Story.*

Week 3

The 'Americanisation' of Shakespeare: Shakespeare as a cultural commodity

Exercise: Ask students to list the qualities that make Shakespeare 'British' and then examine the universal qualities of his plays that make them internationally relevant. How has the most 'British' of authors become so universally accepted? Has film been the main, modern vehicle?

Youth in Shakespeare: How 'youth' is represented in modern adaptations

Exercise: Romeo and Juliet would have been in their early teens. Discuss whether Shakespeare provides a more positive image of teens than current genres such as the teen comedy.

Exercise: Analysis of key-sequences: *10 Things I Hate About You* (Gil Junger, US, 1999). What advantages and disadvantages does referencing Shakespeare provide to a filmmaker?

Week 4

Gender issues and comedy in Shakespeare

Exercise: Recent comedies like *It's a Boy Girl Thing* (Nick Hurran, UK/Canada, 2006) take inspiration from the gender-bending of Shakespearean comedies. Do we laugh with men and at women in these texts? Are they biased in their gender representations? Who come off best or worst in the comedy?

How is the use of humour communicated through dialogue, set-scenes and narrative moments?

Exercise: Analysis of key sequences: *She's the Man* (Andy Fickman, US, 2006): How would the film change if we altered the gender of the main star and imagined a male pretending to be a female? Would it work as well?

Week 5

Issues of clash of creative 'cultures' and low/high culture debate

Exercise: Organise a debate about the merits of theatre and cinema, play and film: Which has the greater cultural influence? Which carries more cultural value?

Teaching sci-fi – page and screen (see pp78–86)

Week 1

The literary foundation of sci-fi – H G Wells and Jules Verne

Exercise: Science fiction writing first appeared in the late 19th century during a period of social and technological upheaval. *Discuss*: Has sci-fi lost its way from its controversial and challenging beginnings?

Written work: What would provide modern audiences with the 'shock' value that came from the original stories?

The generic conventions of sci-fi – plots/characters/narrative elements

Exercise: Choose sci-fi hybrids such as *Wild, Wild West* (Barry Sonnenfeld, US, 1999), *Westworld* (Michael Crichton, US, 1973), *Star Wars* (George Lucas, US, 1977): Is there an argument that each is more of a Western than a sci-fi text? What filmic elements tilt the balance?

Week 2

Mise en scène – constructing the future

Exercise: Watch a behind-the-scene documentary on the DVD of a film such as *The Matrix* (Andy and Larry Wachowski, US/Australia, 1999), focusing on the use of special effects in constructing *mise en scène*.

Character construction – the role of the hero/saviour in sci-fi

Exercise: Many sci-fi films adopt religious iconography in the construction of heroes. Examine this iconography in *The Matrix*. Is it exploitative? Are the directors respectful of the imagery they use? Or is religion just another reference in the postmodern world of sci-fi? Is technology represented a new saviour?

Exercise: Analysis of key-sequences in *The Matrix*. Compare and contrast them with sequences from films *Dark City* (Alex Proyas, US/Australia, 1998) or *Thirteenth Floor* (Joseph Rusnak, US/Germany, 1999). How do sci-fi texts influence each other? Steal from one another?

Week 3

An influential sci-fi franchise: *The Terminator* series (James Cameron and Jonathan Mostow, US, 1984–2003)

Exercise: Analysis of key sequences in *Terminator 3: The Rise of the Machines* (Jonathan Mostow, US, 2003). What issues does the film raise in its portrayal of women? Masculinity? Technology? What is its vision of the future? Is it bleak or positive about humanity?

Week 4

Female characters and their roles in sci-fi, eg the role of Trinity (*The Matrix*) or Sarah Connor (*Terminator*)

Exercise: Analyse sequences featuring these two women. Discuss: To what extent to representations of women in films such as these challenge or reinforce contemporary perceptions of women?

Week 5

Political messages in sci-fi

Exercise: Analysis of key-sequences – *The Day After Tomorrow* (Roland Emmerich, US, 2004). Post-September 11th, are there any political messages in the destruction of cityscapes?

Ask students to identify other sci-fi films that reflect contemporary political concerns.

Exercise: Compare *The Day after Tomorrow* with Al Gore's *An Inconvenient Truth* (Davis Guggenheim, US, 2006). Which is the more effective in conveying a political or social message? Is sci-fi film a good vehicle for such messages?

Week 6

Exercise: Ask students to prepare a pitch for their own sci-fi film idea and present it to the class. Choose the most successful one and develop strategies for making the film.

Introducing cinema from other cultures – Japanese cinema (see pp67–75)

Week 1

Introduction to Japanese cinema

History of Japanese film – link to Japanese theatre traditions

Contrast presentational techniques with representational Western tradition

Exercise: Ask students to research the role of the *benshi* in early Japanese cinema and then provide a *benshi* commentary for a silent-film extract (or a sound film without a soundtrack); students should reinterpret the images for the audience.

Week 2

Introduction to the samurai film – samurai as a symbol of Japanese culture. Post-war Japan – east vs west; tradition vs modernisation

Kurosawa – key-sequences from *Seven Samurai* (Akira Kurosawa, Japan, 1954)

Discussion of style and content; links with modern Hollywood action film; compare with sequences from contemporary Japanese samurai film, eg *The Twilight Samurai* (Yoji Yamada, Japan, 2003) and Western versions, eg *The Last Samurai* (Edward Zwick, US, 2003)

Exercise: Draw up a list of the key features of the film samurai. How are these features used by Japanese and Western filmmakers? What do they tell us about different views of Japan?

Week 3

Introduction to anime: links to manga

Akira – establishing the conventions of anime. Links to Japanese culture – late 20th/21st century

Surrealism and expressionism, rather than linear structures

Studio Ghibli – *Princess Monoke* (Hayao Miyazaki, Japan, 1997), *Spirited Away* (Hayao Miyazaki, Japan, 2002). Sequences and discussions of themes/values. Differences to Western animation

Exercise: Produce your own storyboard for the opening sequence of a new Japanese animated film. Choose your genre and explain how you have adopted or adapted conventions to make it relevant to a Western audience.

Spirited Away

Week 4

Screening: *Shall We Dance* (Masayuki Suo, Japan, 1996)

Key themes – family, individuality, social convention and repression

Form and style – contrast with a US remake

Exercise: Analysis of key sequences.

Week 5

Screening: *Dark Water* (Hideo Nakata, Japan, 2002)

Key themes – family, motherhood, disintegration of social structures

Form and style – contrast with US remake

Exercise: Analysis of key sequences.

Schemes of work

Week 6

Representations of Japan in film; common elements and key differences to Western representations

Changing views of Japanese culture

Popularity of Japanese film and popular culture with young audiences

Essay: In what ways does Japanese film teach us about key messages and values in Japanese society?

Teaching film

1 | Teaching issues

Pedagogy

There are a number of reasons for using film texts in the classroom:

1. the study of the films themselves as objects in their own right;
2. as specific examples to illustrate general ideas about the form and style of the medium;
3. as secondary texts, to enhance our understanding of a primary object of study (eg film versions of novels, films by a writer or director being studied);
4. as historical or cultural documents, offering information about an important time or social movement or set of beliefs.

Anyone teaching film should have a sense of why film texts are being used, and it should be equally evident to students what they are expected to 'do' with any given film text. Clear aims and objectives are welcome in any lesson plan, but it is especially important that when film is used in the classroom, students understand that academic consumption is different from the experience of film in leisure. Whether focusing on small sequences or entire films, students should be given a rationale and distinct tasks to carry out during their viewing and study. This may involve taking notes, completing worksheets or focusing on specific elements in order to contribute to discussion later. Whatever the task, it unambiguously signals that the student needs to be consciously involved in the consumption of the text.

Technology

Some time and investment is needed to ensure that classroom screening facilities are adequate. The most basic screening set-up will probably be a DVD player and TV set, although the limited size of TV screens will not be ideal for groups of 25–30 students. If you are still using VHS, make sure that your VHS player has four recording heads and a jog and shuttle function, so that it is possible to pause sequences with a visible frame and to find individual frames easily. DVD offers the teacher much greater clarity of image, more facilities for searching through films and perfect freeze-framing, although menu systems and complex picture or sound options can catch you out if you are not confident with the technology. Many modern classrooms have made the TV redundant with a mixture of technologies such as DVD-compatible PCs and data projectors, so that moving images can be projected onto screens and whiteboards, creating bigger, clearer pictures for classes. However, you may need to consider investing in an external speaker set-up, since data projectors generally have only rudimentary sound facilities. Don't forget to consider the environment in planning the screening space. Even the most expensive set-up will be nullified if the sun is shining on the screen while you are trying to show films, so invest in decent blinds or blackout curtains if necessary.

Choice of texts

One of the attractions of teaching film is the massive amount of choice of texts on offer. Of course, the films that you choose will be determined by the topics to be covered and the concepts and ideas that you wish to generate. Later in the guide, there are examples of films which we have used in class to good effect and there are many more eminently suitable films available. However, a number of general points should be considered in making your choice. One of the most obvious issues is classification. The age of your audience should by and large determine which films are suitable. It would be inadvisable to study 18-certificated films with a class of 15- and 16-year-olds, even though many will no doubt have watched this class of film. (If necessary, you can use carefully selected extracts of these films to illustrate specific points.)

Contemporary examples are likely to be more popular with the students than older films. However, it may be more difficult to elicit an academic response. Films from outside the students' immediate frame of reference normally require contextualisation in terms of form and content to ensure that they get the most out of them. Initial reactions are often negative – in one of my classes a student told me that they couldn't understand a word of Howard Hawks' 1933 gangster film *Scarface* (US) because the film was in black and white. On the other hand, with proper preparation and good teaching, students are often surprised by and appreciative of the sophistication of products from other eras. The same point can be made for films from outside the US and UK industries. Although students' reactions to subtitles and alien cultural references may be initially hostile, it is often worth persevering in order to demonstrate to students that there are alternatives to the dominant styles established by Hollywood filmmakers. Once again, preparation and appropriate contexts are the keys to success.

Scarface

2 | Methodologies

Textual analysis

The most common and accessible form of engagement with the moving image in an academic environment is close textual analysis. At its most fundamental, this approach to a film sequence involves making students aware of how filmmakers control the various key elements of form and content to create meaning for their audiences. The ubiquity of textual analysis as a methodology at every level of film study owes much to the influence of semiotics in 20th-century cultural philosophy and specifically to the work of French philosopher, Roland Barthes. Barthes revisited the ideas of Swiss linguist Ferdinand de Saussure to show that language does not have a direct connection to the reality it describes, but rather functions as an arbitrary set of signs in which meaning is created by the relationship between the choices that a speaker has at any given time (the *langue* or syntagmatic dimension) and the specific words that they choose (the *parole* or paradigmatic dimension). Barthes was able to demonstrate that language was only one of a myriad of sign systems which surround us and help to make sense of reality for us and went on to analyse many elements of our culture such as fashion and photography through semiotic methods.

GCSE-level students need not be troubled by the development of semiotics in order to appreciate how valuable it is as a method of analysis. However, there are a number of key distinctions which will help their learning. First, students need to be shown that the form and the style of a moving image sequence contribute as much to its meaning as its content. This is not necessarily a straightforward point to grasp, particularly as most students will have become accustomed to watching Hollywood films whose dominant styles are based upon transparency and fluidity for their impact. In order to facilitate this process, students need to be taught the 'grammar' of film:

- camerawork (shot selection, camera angles and camera movement)
- other aspects of *mise en scène* (sets, locations, key props, costumes etc)
- lighting
- sound
- editing.

More detail on these elements can be found in the next section.

Concentrate on short, carefully selected sequences and ask students to apply their new understanding by focusing on one aspect at a time first. You can then introduce all the different technical elements in order for students to understand film's formal qualities. With time students should be able to show how form and content combine to create specific meanings for audiences. In practice, students can pick up on the visual elements – camerawork and other aspects of *mise en scène* – fairly quickly, but may struggle to understand and articulate their knowledge of editing or sound a little more. Plenty of guidance and practice with clear examples will make the process of analysis seem less mystifying.

Textual analysis exercises can take a number of forms with your classes:

- A whole group exercise, directed and focused by the teacher, in which students contribute and build on each other's ideas to create a collective analysis of a sequence. This can be difficult with a large class and it is not easy to record students' feedback in a meaningful form.
- As a class exercise, with the class broken up into groups and given a specific focus for the analysis (ie one group analysing the camerawork, one group analysing the sound and so on). Each group feeds back to the class in turn and then everybody is encouraged to discuss the relationships between the various elements.
- In groups or as individuals, students produce a textual analysis of a short sequence to present to the class, who may then respond with additions or alternative analyses. If students have access to IT, presentations can be constructed with screen grabs and a slideshow package such as Microsoft PowerPoint to focus on certain elements.

Students should also be encouraged to grasp the difference between denotation and connotation as levels of meaning. Denotation is the first level of meaning – the literal, surface meaning of a particular sign. The second level of meaning, connotation, arises from the associations and evaluations of that sign through its particular position within our culture. Of course, there is every chance that these associations are numerous and potentially contradictory. Barthes identified the 'polysemy' of signs, their potential for carrying multiple meanings, as one of the defining features of any sign system. Good textual analysis should make students aware of the possibility of alternative meanings.

Ideological analysis

It will sometimes be necessary to move beyond an analysis of how the text creates meanings to an examination of the importance of those meanings in constructing a film's values and belief systems. This can be another difficult step for students since often these value systems are so deeply rooted within particular cultures that they appear natural or 'common sense'. There are a number of accessible ways to begin this process:

- Focus on a particular character in a film and try to draw up a list of the values that are important to the character (make sure that students concentrate on values and don't just produce a character sketch). Think about the way in which the film encourages audiences to endorse or criticise these values through its content and form. What alternative value systems are set up through other characters?

- Look specifically at the end sequence of the film. In what ways are characters rewarded or punished for their actions? What kinds of values do these characters stand for? What does this tell us about the film's value system as a whole?

- Identify a particular area in which the students can look for evidence of tension or conflict in the value systems (eg law and order, individuals and the community, religion, gender or racial representations). Focus on the different values presented and the ways that these are 'offered' to the audience. How does the film attempt to prioritise certain value systems? How are other values criticised or marginalised?

In order to consider these issues, it is important that students think about not only the content, but the way in which this is presented through formal and stylistic features, hence the importance of textual analysis as a basic skill.

Contextual analysis

Contextual analysis uses both textual and ideological analysis to demonstrate how a specific film or sequence derives its meaning from its relationship to other similar or related texts. This kind of exercise is limited if simply used to generate long lists of similarities and differences between a particular film and others in a related group. However, students can be encouraged to explain and evaluate the significance of these patterns in order to shed light on particular examples. A contextual analysis can be done with:

- Films by a specific director/producer/writer. Despite the collective, industrial nature of film production, it is often possible to locate common themes, values or visual styles in the work of individual filmmakers.

- Films based in a specific culture and a specific era. These will often reveal strong connections to the key issues of that place and time.

- Films based on the same source material.

- Films in the same genre. Genre study is probably the most common kind of contextual study, but is laden with problems concerning the definition of genre and how both filmmakers and audiences understand the concept. Nevertheless, it should be possible to show how generic templates (in terms of iconography, character types, narratives, visual styles and so on) are either recycled or redefined by individual film texts.

Contextual analysis can be a daunting prospect because of the amount of material that needs to be covered in order to draw firm and accurate conclusions from your analysis. However, it should be possible to select material that will allow students to make clear links between the texts, as long as they have been given comprehensive instructions as to the nature of the comparisons to be made.

Research

At some point, it will be helpful to set tasks to encourage students to generate their own learning materials. Student research can be fraught with difficulty, particularly if the activity set is vague in nature or outcome. It is important that you convey a clear idea of the kinds of information that students should 'discover', directing them in the early stages of their research so that they are able to generate initial material and do not become discouraged by the task. You must also give instructions as to how the research should be presented and assessed. When teaching film, there are some well-established research tasks you can set, concerning:

- production details and histories of specific films;
- biographical details of actors or filmmakers;
- historical accounts of film genre development;
- comparative research into various versions of a single text.

The type of research will depend on the resources available. At the very least, a small library of key books, journals and magazines should be accessible to students, either on permanent display (though likely to disappear over time) or in the form of a book box available on a lesson-by-lesson basis. The bibliography suggests a number of reference books to include in such a research resource. If you have viewing facilities, a DVD library will also be worthwhile, allowing students to access audiovisual material as and when necessary.

The internet, of course, contains a wealth of information, but students need to be taught how to access this, otherwise they can soon be overwhelmed by irrelevant or unsuitable websites. The sites below are often good starting points for general information about specific films:

- <www.imdb.com> the Internet Movie Database;
- <www.filmsite.org> a comprehensive film reference site;
- <www.moviefinder.com> film synopses and listings;
- <www.bfi.org.uk> the BFI's website with links to a wide range of information about films and other educational resources;
- <www.screenonline.org.uk> the BFI's comprehensive resource site for British film.

For more general material, teach your students how to employ search engines as effectively as possible. (You can find a series of tutorials on how to use the Google engine at <www.googleguide.com>.) The ability to focus a search and to sift through found material quickly will ensure that internet research does not bore or distract students. If possible, set out some specific outcomes for the material that is found:

- a presentation to the class, perhaps using a PowerPoint slideshow;
- a research book or dossier;
- a diagrammatic presentation such as a mind map or a timeline.

This will encourage students to use their research productively rather than printing out reams of pages that are never read or digested.

Other approaches

Students' familiarity with and enthusiasm for film as a medium can be a powerful tool in setting up a film study task. Careful handling can ensure productive use of this particular resource. Below are examples of student-centred activities which could be adapted to a range of films and issues. For the relevant worksheets go to the home page for this book at <www.bfi.org.uk/tms> and enter username **filmgcse@bfi.org.uk**; password: **gc1603fi**.

Make my film (Worksheet 1)

In small groups, students develop a film pitch based upon their study of the science fiction genre. They come up with a narrative, key character roles and a unique selling point for their film. They should discuss how the film would be appropriate for its target audience (that is, the ideal audience for the product) and how it might be most effectively marketed to that audience.

Page to screen (Worksheet 2)

As above, but groups compete to win the rights to turn a specific novel or play into a film. Students can focus upon key areas of the text which must be retained for the film version and decide which parts might be cut or adapted. They can make suggestions for the key creative personnel – screenwriter, director, stars – and justify these choices. Debate could also identify the qualities of the text likely to suffer in a film version and those which might benefit or be improved.

Studio executives (Worksheet 3)

This role-play exercise requires a little preparation and some research by students. Given a limited budget and a list of possible expenditure options, students need to decide how they will invest their money to create a roster of films for a twelve-month release period. Some research into box-office lists should indicate which genres are currently in vogue and indicate release patterns for specific times of the year, to be combined with the students' own knowledge. The exercise can be tailored to suit particular study topics. For example, studios can be based in competing film markets (European, US, Indian) or attempting to create a brand for themselves (blockbuster film, niche product). Students need to be prepared to explain the criteria used to make their decisions and the factors that might undermine potential success.

Censorship debate (Worksheet 4)

Students are given specific roles to play within the debate – filmmakers, studio executives, British Board of Film Censorship (BBFC) examiners, members of lobby groups such as MediaWatch or NVLA (National Viewers and Listeners Association), politicians, parents and so on – along with some guidance as to the perspective that they will represent. With a little research and preparation, they should offer a brief account of their viewpoint and then be prepared to justify their beliefs in a general discussion.

Top fives (Worksheet 5)

Set the focus in order to tie in with the area of study and ask students to draw up a list of their 'Top five…' Steven Spielberg films; comic book heroes on film; trailers; Shakespeare texts on film; and so on.

Students must be prepared to justify their choices and to explain the criteria they applied to rank the films. In groups, you could even ask students to present their choices in the mode of a TV special (along the lines of Channel 4 or Five's regular *Top Ten…* list shows) with a presenter, pundits and clips from the films chosen.

Practical work

The nature of film study is such that the more abstract concerns of analysis are never far removed from the concrete issues of production. Unsurprisingly then, practical work can be one of the most important classroom tools in increasing students' understanding of film as a conveyor of meaning. Practical assignments in the classroom will be dependent upon your school's resources (cameras, sound equipment, editing facilities), the time you have available and suitable space. Success will also be linked to your own confidence as a practitioner or how much technical support you have. There is no point in sending students off with expensive equipment until they know how to make the best use of its features in order to create a shot or sequence with a clear filmic purpose. Having said this, practical work does not have to be limited by technology or technological know-how; we have listed a number of suggestions for how practical work might enhance the study of film in the classroom, covering various degrees of sophistication:

- Storyboarding is an effective way for students to demonstrate their understanding of film languages and conventions without the need for time-consuming shooting and editing. Artistic skill is not necessarily a prerequisite; digital still cameras can be used to recreate shots, as well as indicate knowledge of camerawork and other aspects of *mise en scène* such as lighting. Alternatively, software such as FrameForge can be generate digital storyboards with a little training.

- Film-marketing materials – posters, screenshots, DVD covers, magazine interviews, press releases etc – can help in exploring genre and the role of stars in creating a film's meaning. This can be done in a low-tech way, with a collage-style approach or in a more sophisticated manner with image manipulation and DTP software.
- Video work challenges students to exercise their understanding of film language, by learning to employ the conventions of form and style to express themselves effectively. It is unlikely that they will have the time, energy or expertise to produce their own features, but the production of trailers, opening scenes or short genre sequences all afford excellent opportunities for the fusion of theory and production learning.

For a full examination of the key issues involved in using production exercises in a classroom context, see the BFI's companion text, *Teaching Digital Video Production at GCSE*.

Key books

Graeme Burton *More than Meets the Eye*, Hodder Arnold, 2001
Andrew Goodwyn *English Teaching and the Moving Image*, Routledge, 2003
Nick Lacey *Key Concepts in Media Studies* series, Macmillan, 2000)
James Monaco *How to Read a Film*, OUP, 2000)
David Wharton, Jeremy Grant *Teaching Analysis of Film Language and Production* (*Teaching Film and Media Studies*), BFI, 2006

Websites

Although many of these are A-level based, the resources can be reworked to suit any purpose.
<www.mediaknowall.com> an introduction to standard terms and concepts.
<www.englishandmedia.co.uk> a central hub particularly useful for publications, downloadable resources and connection to the excellent MediaMagazine with much of its content written by teenagers, for teenagers.
<www.mediaed.org.uk> a site that is more academic in tone and also more conscious of the social effect of media usage, production and consumption.
<www.studymedia.co.uk> a site that also draws in the practical aspects.
<www.longroadmedia.com> excellent user friendly site if you are new to the subject and want to have a clear idea of which areas to cover. Its coverage of key concepts (by Chief Examiners who also teach in the college) is highly accessible.
<www.hurtwoodmedia.com> Our own site and therefore perhaps a rather biased recommendation. The Hurtwood can show GCSE students ways forward with coursework in the area of Video/Print and Web.

Studying film

1 | Key concepts

The following paragraphs outline some of the fundamental concepts of film study and the ways in which a knowledge of these can enhance your students' understanding of film. This is not an exhaustive list of concepts and theory by any means, as we have tried to restrict ourselves to those areas of study which have been most productive in our teaching and the students' learning. Nevertheless, we firmly believe that there is little point in overwhelming students with film theory that is only ever regurgitated in half-understood soundbites or irrelevant asides. Effective use of theory in class should be preceded by the question 'Will this help my students to…?'. On the other hand, without some understanding of the academic and conceptual structures which underpin this subject, students are only ever likely to produce superficial or general knowledge-style responses.

above *Psycho*

User name: **filmgcse@bfi.org.uk**   Password: **gc1603fi**

Film language

Like any system of communication, film is dependent upon our familiarity with its rules or 'grammar'. However, outside the classroom this understanding is rarely articulated or considered at a conscious level. The ubiquity of film in our culture encourages us to believe that texts communicate 'naturally' or 'transparently' and the continuity style adopted by most Western filmmakers encourages this lack of attention to the techniques of construction. In order to appreciate how films create meanings for their audiences, students must be able to analyse how the different elements of film language work both in isolation and in conjunction with one another.

Mise en scène

One of the most obvious places to begin the process of analysis is with the *mise en scène*. Although this term has been defined in a variety of ways, it generally refers to the elements involved in the construction of the visual impact of a shot or a sequence. Students can be asked to consider the content of a sequence as well as the formal techniques applied. The elements of *mise en scène* to consider are:

■ Location
The setting of a particular sequence will normally serve a narrative function (for example, a location that acts as an 'arena' in an action-adventure film so that the protagonist and the antagonist can battle each other); and/or a thematic function, implying important values within the film as a whole (the desert and township settings of many Westerns); or, by association, the values of particular characters (the steep mountainside shown in the opening of *Vertical Limit* (Martin Campbell, US, 2000)) immediately indicates the skills of the protagonists, as well as their connection to the 'natural' world of mountaineering.

■ Costume
The demands of genre and verisimilitude go some way towards determining decisions about costume. There also is almost always a degree to which characters are constructed through the connotations of their clothing. For example, the agents in *The Matrix* trilogy (Andy and Larry Wachowski, US, 1999–2003) are made threatening through the appropriation of the uniform of the US home security forces, with their connotations of anonymity and the popular belief that these forces work beyond conventional law.

■ Props
Key props can function as narrative devices in their own right. Hitchcock called these 'McGuffins' since their inherent qualities were less important than their role as a catalyst for narrative events (such as the case of the money which Marion steals from her employer in *Psycho* (Alfred Hitchcock, US, 1960). They may also

Rear Window

serve to impart information about characters. James Stewart's camera in *Rear Window* (Alfred Hitchcock, US, 1954), for example, reveals his profession – he is a photographer – and his main character trait: he is a voyeur.

The above elements of *mise en scène* are normally readily identified and discussed by students who, with encouragement, should be able to move beyond descriptive accounts of their importance.

Try commutation tests to focus students' attention upon how location, costume and props might create meaning within context. These involve replacing key elements with (possibly outlandish) alternatives to imagine what impact this would have on the meanings of a sequence. Alternatively, ask students to create specific sequences or characters for themselves, based on limited narrative information. These can then be compared to the filmmaker's real choices and the differences in meaning discussed.

Camerawork

Students need to be challenged to look beyond the 'obvious' elements of *mise en scène* to the process of construction through technical aspects. The shot is the most fundamental of these and demands that students recognise how the camera is positioned in relation to the action (shot size and shot angle), how it moves in relation to the action (camera movement), and how it is focused in relation to the action.

Worksheet 6 indicates some of the choices available to the filmmaker with regard to shot size, shot angle and camera movement.

These definitions are not precise, though the use of the human figure as a guide to understanding composition is nearly universal. Neither are the meanings of specific shot types 'fixed'. Although generalisations are possible, close-ups serve to emphasise important emotional or psychological qualities in a character, long shots depersonalise and distance us from individuals – the large number of exceptions in a wide variety of examples should remind us that camera use should always be analysed in context.

Focus can direct our attention to particular areas of the frame. Typically, shallow focus presents a figure or an object sharply in the foreground, while backgrounds are difficult to perceive; deep focus offers the viewer detail in all planes of the frame. Focus can be shifted within a single frame by use of a focus pull, which often implies an important relationship between the figures or objects focused upon.

In the classroom

Storyboarding can help students develop an understanding of the function of the camera as part of the *mise en scène*, particularly when they are asked to use the camera to create interest in a sequence which lacks inherent visual impact. A 30-second sequence on boiling an egg or a game of chess focuses attention on the role of camerawork and can be drawn or easily constructed from digital camera stills for added authenticity.

Lighting

Like many aspects of film production, lighting is a sophisticated and demanding process which often goes unnoticed by students. The high-key lighting style of many Hollywood films demands at least three light sources on each of the main actors or elements of a sequence (a main or key light to provide most of the illumination, a fill light to remove obvious areas of shadow and a backlight to ensure that the subject is crisply defined) to provide a well-illuminated, low-contrast scene. The fact that the lighting has to be changed and balanced for each individual camera set-up should indicate how much care goes into creating an ambience which the audience perceives as 'natural'.

Often, lighting serves to reveal psychological or thematic values within sequences, most obviously in those films utilising a low-key lighting set-up. Here, a strong contrast between harder light and dark shadows (similar to the chiaroscuro techniques of fine art) achieves a particular effect. This technique is commonly employed to create mystery and menace in horror films and played a major role in creating the threatening and morally ambiguous urban landscapes of the crime films of the 1940s and 1950s.

Editing

The basic premise of editing – that two shots are joined together in a specific relationship with one another – belies the complexity of ways in which editing can create meanings for audiences. In the very early years of cinema, the Russian filmmaker Kuleshov was able to demonstrate the power of editing through a series of experiments in which he edited the same image of an emotionless actor into a variety of shots including a steaming bowl of broth, a coffin and a young girl playing with a bear. Viewers, influenced by the editing, perceived the expression of the actor to show hunger, grief and love despite the fact that his expression does not change. The ability of editing to create meaning through the juxtaposition of shots, rather than from what we actually see on screen makes it a crucial part of the filmmaking process, but it also makes it one of the elements which students find hardest to analyse and articulate.

Various transitions are possible in the editing process, as indicated in **Worksheet 7**.

In the majority of Hollywood films, the editing process is heavily influenced by the need to retain narrative continuity and follows a system of rules known as continuity editing. Because of our familiarity with the continuity system, we tend to regard the editing as fluid and 'natural'; however, the system works through a series of conventional strategies:

- Spatial continuity: Establishing shots often feature at the beginning of a sequence to delineate important elements of time and space, such as the setting and the spatial relationships of key characters. Re-establishing shots may occur in the middle of sequences if spatial relationships alter significantly.

- Motivated editing: Cutting is dictated by the demands of narrative events. For example, dialogue may determine that we cut back and forth between two speakers in a pattern known as shot/reverse shot. Alternatively, action may determine the pattern of editing, with cuts most often occurring during moments of movement (match on action). Cutting can also serve to represent the points of view of key characters; for example, the eyeline match cuts from a character's glance, to the focus of his attention.

Part 2 | Studying film 1 Key concepts

- Elimination of dead time: Cuts are made to compress time so that key narrative events are retained while the 'unimportant' time between them is removed. The fluidity of action is maintained by changing camera angles or cutting away to a related sequence so that we do not notice the ellipsis. Jump-cuts are a variation of this technique where the ellipsis is made deliberately obvious in order to create impact for an audience

The basis of the continuity system is a production process which adheres rigorously to a 180° rule, ensuring that sequences are shot with a consistent axis of action. **Worksheet 8** illustrates the basics of this system.

Once the principles of editing are understood, the challenge is to motivate students to analyse editing in a meaningful fashion. It may help to ask them to focus on the following questions:

- How is the pace of a sequence affected by its editing? (Conventionally, shots become shorter and cuts more frequent as scenes build to a climax, but there are plenty of exceptions.)
- How does the editing create a point of view in a sequence? Students should examine which characters are given the majority of screen time and which characters seem to motivate the editing most frequently.
- How does the editing distribute narrative information? Does the audience know more than the characters about events that are unfolding? This can create tension, for example, in a sequence where the protagonist enters a warehouse that we have seen is booby-trapped in a cutaway shot. Or are we aligned with particular characters in having key information withheld from us, as in a horror sequence where the arrival of the threat or the monster will take both character and audience by surprise.

Students might also be directed to look for examples of filmmakers breaking continuity rules and inferring why they did so.

In the classroom

- Basic editing techniques can be introduced with simple exercises, involving still images from a sequence which groups can arrange in order to create a narrative. Each group should explain their decisions and suggest how the sequence might continue.

- Modern PCs using the Windows XP OS have a Windows Moviemaker facility, allowing students to carry out basic drop-and-drag tasks with film clips. If these can be prepared in advance, this is an excellent way to involve students in making decisions about editing.

▶▶

◄◄

- Cheap editing packages such as the Pinnacle system on PCs or iMovie on Macs should allow for more sophisticated tasks. Filming and editing a conversation or another two-person event will help to show students the issues created by continuity editing and the 180° rule.

Sound

Although there is a tendency to privilege visual modes in film analysis, the importance of sound in the process of making meaning should not be underestimated. The pervasiveness of sound in film is such that moments of genuine silence are both rare and startling in their impact. Conversely, students need to be aware of how sound is being used to support, or perhaps subvert, the visual meanings of a sequence.

- Diegetic sound (sound that is generated from within the world of the narrative events, the diegesis) may refer to the dialogue, the ambient sounds employed to create a sense of place, or specific sound effects that have narrative significance. Diegetic sound can be synchronous, that is, linked to a source that we can see on screen or asynchronous, emerging from outside the frame.
- Non-diegetic sound is imposed from outside of the diegesis, most commonly in the form of a soundtrack or, possibly, a narration or voice-over.

In the classroom

A common technique for emphasising the importance of sound involves watching sequences with the sound removed and asking students to indicate which sound should be present and why. On the other hand, it can be equally effective to remove the visual elements to indicate how powerfully sound can communicate in its own right. The Mines of Moria sequence from *The Lord of the Rings: The Fellowship of the Ring* (Peter Jackson, US/NZ, 2001) is a fantastic example of how much sound contributes to the mood, characterisation and narrative of film.

Messages and values

One of the common criticisms of Hollywood films by academics is that they offer contrived happy endings, which falsely impose a moral order upon the world. The criticism seems churlish, since film is only one of a whole host of narrative entertainments that rely upon 'happy ever afters' for effect. It is clear that almost all films have a major theme or message of some sort to offer their audiences, whether it is the privileging of good over evil, law and justice over crime, or love over adversity. The resolution or climax of the narrative is the moment that this message is ultimately revealed, although any film will have been constantly working to position its audiences to expect and be satisfied by that message. However, the film's meanings are not completely constrained by its overall message and much of the impact of film comes from the way in which it articulates this message through the manipulation of a large number of different, possibly conflicting, demographics. Some examples of these relate to:

- gender;
- gational and ethnic identities;
- age;
- sex and sexuality;
- physical abilities;
- religion and morality;
- family and community.

An approach to teaching messages and values

Encouraging students to think about the ways in which characters are represented as part of these value systems is a good way to begin the process of analysing messages and values. Begin with still images of the key characters to discuss how casting, costume and props contribute to our understanding of them. Then, short, well-chosen sequences can be shown to support initial ideas by demonstrating how formal features – camerawork, editing, sound – build on these meanings to create coherent character models.

Students should also be asked to consider how the film privileges certain characters or groups of characters, while marginalising others. Again, this will be achieved both through *mise en scène* and other technical features and some good close analysis should demonstrate how this occurs. By creating a hierarchy of characters, it should then be possible to discuss why the value systems associated with particular characters are consequently privileged or marginalised by the film as a whole.

▶▶

The following exercises can help with this process. Ask students to:

- Produce a mind map of all the qualities and values associated with protagonist and antagonist of the film you are studying. Discuss how these qualities are significant within the genre of the film. See **Worksheet 9**.

- Write or storyboard some 'deleted scenes' from the film you are studying, which make obvious the key values of the characters. Discuss why filmmakers do not often resort to such obvious methods of signposting these values. See **Worksheet 10**.

- Try commutation exercises in which various elements of protagonists' and antagonists' construction (casting, costume, key props, key locations and so on) are swapped around. What effect would it have on the meanings of the film?

The difficulty in analysing the messages and values of mainstream films is often that the values are so strongly linked with dominant value systems that they appear natural, and therefore closed to challenge or debate. It is worthwhile introducing the concepts of ideology and hegemony in a digestible format so that you can explore how 'common sense' is simply a value system that the majority of us have accepted.

Audiences

Any study of film will be made more rewarding with an understanding of the role the audience has in making meaning from texts. Both Media and English teachers can use their students' self-awareness as audiences and their experience of film watching as well as a range of readings on the subject.

The importance of the audience might be considered in three related arenas:

1 Target audiences

All films are constructed with an 'ideal' audience in mind – those for whom the construction of the film hold the greatest relevance or appeal and who are therefore most likely to pay to see it in the cinema or at home. Hollywood blockbusters need to target a large audience in order to recoup the massive costs of production and marketing; niche films can afford to target more specific audiences as they generally cost less to produce. The actual audience for these films is likely to come from a variety of social groups, many of which fall outside the target demographic. However, some concept of the intended or ideal audience will help students to understand the choices that filmmakers have made in the content and form of their product.

2 Context of consumption

The way in which a film is watched has an important effect upon the meanings that it generates. A film is watched differently in the cinema than at home on DVD or TV which, in turn, is different to the ways that it is watched in the classroom. The differences are both environmental and cultural – the darkened auditorium, large screen and focused audience of the cinema demand that we experience film more immediately and with less control than in a home environment, where we can pause, fast-forward and skip scenes and do other things at the same time. To a large degree, the way in which the audience consume the film is beyond the control of filmmakers, but it is worth considering how a film attempts to cater for or mitigate against different contexts of reception. For example, the spectacle scenes of a major Hollywood film such as *Spider-Man* (Sam Raimi, US, 2002) are most effectively consumed on the big screen; on the other hand, a film such as *Memento* (Christopher Nolan, US, 2000), with its complex narrative structure and time scheme seems as if it were made with the home-viewing experience and the ability to rewind in mind.

Memento

3 Spectatorship

This complex area attempts to account for the ways in which audiences interpret the messages and values of film in the process of consumption. Early research into the possible relationships between films and their audiences, such as the Payne Fund studies carried out in the US in the 1930s, tended to regard the audience as a mass entity who were easily manipulated into assimilating the messages and values of films they watched. These assumptions about the audience crystallised into a model of audience behaviour known as the Effects model.

During the 1970s, structuralist thinkers developed a similarly deterministic view of the cinema spectator out of a brew of linguistic, Marxist and psychoanalytical theory. One of the most important aspects of the 'apparatus' of cinema was its ability to position, or interpellate, spectators in such a way that they were unable to resist the reactionary social representations that were invariably offered. Laura Mulvey's discussion of the cinema spectator being positioned to watch film with a 'male gaze' is one of the more persistent manifestations of this view.

A more flexible construction of the spectator has emerged from the disciplines of Cultural Studies. This way of understanding suggests that the social formation of the individual members of the audience, as well as their relative level of media literacy, will allow them to produce a number of potential 'readings' of a film. A preferred reading implies that the viewer has accepted the intended messages and values, while a negotiated reading suggests that there is some tension in the viewer's relationship with the film in which some value systems are accepted, while others may be challenged or rejected. An oppositional reading is one in which the film's messages and values are recognised but rejected by the audience. The variety of readings implied in this model is tempered by the ways in which film's formal qualities (such as its relationship to genre) work to restrict potential meanings, as well as the shared social background of many film audiences.

Producers

Film study is always improved by offering students some insight into the specific demands of film production, since the development of film form and content is inevitably linked to the production context and whether the film is targeted at specific audiences with a view to making as much profit as possible, or whether it is primarily an art film, for example.

In the next section (pp45–75) there is a more detailed account of various film industries and the development of national cinemas.

Narrative

Given the ubiquity of narrative in our lives, it is unsurprising that film has developed principally as a medium of storytelling. The link between film and narrative is so strong that students rarely appreciate that film can be organised around alternative structures and ideas.

In the classroom

It can be an interesting exercise to screen an extract from a non-narrative film (eg *Un Chien Andalou* (Luis Buñuel and Salvador Dali, France, 1929) or *8½* (Federico Fellini, Italy, 1963)) and to ask students to 'explain' it. Most commonly, they will attempt to impose a narrative on events, grasping for any evidence of familiar story structures in the process.

In order to analyse how film narratives work, it is worth drawing a distinction between the story and the plot of a film.

- The story refers to all the events in a narrative: those that are presented and those that are inferred by the audience. As such the story may consist of events that we never see (eg Ethan Edwards stealing Confederate gold before returning to his brother's homestead in *The Searchers* (John Ford, US, 1956)).

The Searchers

■ The plot refers to those events which are presented to us directly in the film. These events are part of the story, but do not necessarily represent everything we need to know.

A film narrative is built out of the dynamic set up between its plot and its story.

A number of different models or theories are commonly used when attempting to show that narrative is not an arbitrary sequence of events but a set of predetermined structures applied make sense of an apparently disordered universe. Many of these models have their basis in literary criticism; the inherent qualities of each model are less important than the fact that students are being encouraged to think about why these structures are important.

Todorov's widely adopted model of narrative structure suggests that there are five major phases in the development of a narrative. This is a simplified, but helpful breakdown:

1. a state of normality or equilibrium;
2. a disruption to the equilibrium by some kind of force;
3. a recognition of this disruption and a period of disequilibrium;
4. the application of a further force in order to resolve the disequilibrium;
5. a return to equilibrium, though different from the initial state.

Ask students to apply this structure to film narratives that they know well and to feed back their findings. It should be possible to demonstrate that the majority of mainstream Hollywood films fit neatly into this model, although students may find that equilibrium is implied in the story, rather than shown in the plot. For example, *Star Wars* (George Lucas, US, 1977) plunges us into the middle of a galactic conflict. It should also be possible to show that each stage of this structure can be genre-specific, so that the destabilising force of an action film is likely to be physical violence and destruction, while in a romantic comedy it is likely to be an emotional event, such as falling in love with someone unattainable. With sufficient knowledge, students may be able to find examples of films that do not fit this structure; independent and art films, for example, often snub the convenience of a return to equilibrium at the end of a narrative.

One fundamental difference between the narratives of novels and those of films is that of narration. While many printed narratives assume an omniscient narrator who allows us to see and hear what we need to make sense of events, another common strategy is to employ a first-person narrator (or several) in order to create a dynamic between unfolding events and subjective viewpoints. Film, at first glance, appears to work almost exclusively in the former mode, using an omniscient style in order to place the audience into an objective viewing position. Although the existence of the point-of-view shot suggests a filmic equivalent of the first-person perspective, only one feature film – *The Lady in the Lake* (Robert Montgomery, US, 1947) – has ever adopted this technique for its entire length and then with only limited success. However, it is clear that films do create perspective through a variety of techniques – camera, editing, sound – and it is worth establishing with the students whose viewpoint we, as the audience, are most closely aligned with (and how this alignment is achieved). Students can be introduced to the idea that the characters are commonly those with whom they share key value systems. Alternatively, filmmakers may choose to create proximity with characters whose values are clearly at odds with 'normal' behaviour – Napoleon Dynamite in Jared Hess's film (US, 2004) of the same name for example – encouraging the audience to examine what constitutes our understanding of 'normal' in the first place. This kind of study works productively when linked with a discussion of a film's messages and values (see p32).

Character

Film characters, as we have already seen, are most usefully thought of as constructions. The filmmaker, unlike the writer, rarely has the luxury of time or narration to build the kind of psychological subtlety into their characters that we are accustomed to in novels. In film narratives, characters tend to be given defining qualities or traits which determine the role that they play in the narrative, while creating the illusion of personality. Their traits will be well signalled and concomitant with the demands of narrative cause and effect. Major characters tend to have collections of traits (occasionally in tension with one another if a character is to be regarded as 'complex' – Superman must balance his responsibilities as a saviour of mankind, with his personal desires, such as his love for Lois); minor characters are given one or two significant traits which 'explain' their role (Superman's antagonist, Lex Luthor's ambition and megalomania, for example).

When looking at film adaptations of novels, it is rewarding to examine the processes through which characters are transferred from the page to the screen. Although this modification is often referred to as 'bringing a character to life', in fact it often entails a simplification of a character's psychological state so that they can be 'understood' by a film audience and it is one of the reasons that readers often feel short-changed by film versions of their favourite books.

In the classroom

Focus on a particular genre, and ask your students to create a number of characters for a new film. They should identify:

- aspects of physical appearance;
- elements of props and costumes;
- character traits;
- casting possibilities.

Then show, diagrammatically, how the characters would be related to one another through the narrative structure of a film in this genre. See **Worksheet 13**.

Genre

From the early days of Hollywood filmmaking, it was apparent to film studios and filmmakers that, in order to sell their products, films needed to provide a balance between the familiar (those elements that audiences looked for and enjoyed while watching a film) and the unfamiliar (the unique, different or challenging elements which differentiated one film from another). One obvious way of achieving this kind of balance was through a star system – audiences who enjoyed Charlie Chaplin films would return to subsequent products, but these needed to vary sufficiently in terms of narrative, stunts and gags to offer a unique experience. (The role of the star system in Hollywood will be discussed in more detail in the next chapter.)

Another key strategy was to organise the production and marketing of films in terms of different 'types' of product, so that successful formulae could be efficiently recycled and adapted by filmmakers and sold with the minimum of marketing effort to established audiences.

It is common to think about genre as a system of categories or pigeonholes into which films fall by employing a repertoire of familiar elements. While there is truth in this method of looking at film, it belies the complexity of the ways in which genre functions as a set of relationships that exists between the film industry, individual filmmakers and film audiences.

The film industry, dependent upon producing profitable products for its continued existence, frequently takes key decisions about which projects can be undertaken (or greenlighted) and how much money will be invested in those products based upon the individual film's relationship to a genre. The success of a particular genre film will often facilitate the production of similar types of film. Thus, the runaway success of *The Lord of the Rings* trilogy has led to the production of fantasy-film franchises based on CS Lewis's *The Chronicle of Narnia* and Philip Pullman's *His Dark Materials* trilogy. Conversely, poor reception for individual films can lead genres to stagnate or disappear; despite a brief resurgence in the late 1980s and early 1990s, the Western is no longer the staple film formula that it was for much of the Hollywood studio system era of the 1940s and 1950s. As such, genre exists as a kind of blueprint, which precedes and programmes industry production. It is frequently written of contemporary Hollywood that it is overly dependent upon genre models to pattern production and to reduce the risk of financial failure. The 'high-concept' film, whose premise relies upon a spectacular but simple articulation of genre conventions is often regarded as the nadir of 1980s' Hollywood (*Top Gun* (Tony Scott, US, 1986) – *Rocky* (John G Avildsen, US, 1976) crossed with *An Officer and a Gentleman* (Taylor Hackford, US, 1982), plus jet fighters!). The hybrid product mixes together compatible (or sometimes not so compatible) genres in the hope of widening a film's potential target market.

The creative and technical choices of every element of film production are also determined by the filmmakers' (conscious or unconscious) understanding of genre. This understanding serves as a benchmark for filmmakers who must position their product in relation to previous related films, by reusing some conventions, ignoring others or possibly innovating by introducing elements which themselves may become conventions for future filmmakers. This 'play' with genre conventions is most obvious at the level of a film's iconography, but also functions through character types, narrative structures, audiovisual style and the themes and values of the film.

Film marketing (a crucial part of any film release, involving budgets which run into millions of dollars) will focus their campaign on a film's genre to target audiences who are familiar with, or fans of, particular genres. This can lead to difficulties for filmmakers who innovate or challenge genre models dramatically, since most of the major distributors use genre in their marketing strategy. The initially limited success of the cult teen film *Donnie Darko* (Richard Kelly, US, 2001) was in part due to the reluctance of the US distributors to sell a film which mixed a coming-of-age-narrative, with science-fiction iconography and character types that seemed to belong in horror films. Alternatively, film marketing may emphasise particular generic elements at the expense of others in order to target profitable audience groups. Wes Craven's *Scream* (US, 1996) was marketed unambiguously to teenage audiences as a horror film (with a title change from *Scary Movie* to emphasise the point) even though it is arguably a thriller or a whodunit, lacking any supernatural or spiritual dimension.

Scream

The information that an audience receives about a film prior to viewing it – whether through the specific marketing or more indirect forms of promotion such as interviews, word of mouth or merchandising – almost always entails a generic context for the consumption of a film. John Ellis has suggested the notion of a *narrative image*, composed from a general understanding of genre and specific foreknowledge of any given film, that furnishes a series of expectations for the viewing. The way in which films achieve a balance between the fulfilment and disruption of these expectations defines both the enjoyment and the meaning of the film for an audience.

Academic study of film has built further on these institutional discourses of genre. By studying groups of films which seem to share generic characteristics, it has been possible for academics to gain a broader understanding of the underlying messages and values of particular genres. Will Wright and Jim Kitses both produced groundbreaking studies of the Western genre, based on the notion that a wide variety of apparently disparate Western films actually shared very similar ideological structures, often examining the role of the individual and his or her relationship to a community. More recently, Thomas Schatz has examined genre in terms of the predictable cycles of development through which genre films appear to pass. Interestingly, Schatz uses his study of genre to claim that ultimately all film genres can be located within two fundamental categories or ur-genres. A table based on Schatz's discussion of genres of order and genres of integration can be found in **Worksheet 14**.

In the classroom

Research the categorisation criteria adopted by online DVD sales sites such as <www.amazon.co.uk> or <www.play.com> and discuss the features which determine how films end up in particular categories. Who is making these decisions? How much is the audience's understanding of genre determined by the popularity of various films and the need to make money?

Authorship

The question of authorship in film is by no means straightforward. While related forms of creative expression such as the novel, play or artwork generally emerge from individual endeavour and can be attributed fairly easily to a single creator, the collaborative nature of film production complicates the process of identifying a single author. Most frequently, the director is considered to be the most important creative influence. However, a number of other key personnel could potentially lay claim to shaping the creative success of a film:

- Producer:

In the Hollywood studio system, the producer was unambiguously regarded as 'responsible' for a film's production and would have hired or contracted a director only for the duration of the shooting period. Pre- and post-production work would have been overseen by the producer. The collapse of the system changed the relationship between producers and directors, although there remain a number of Hollywood producers whose 'style' seems to transcend the different directors with which they work, for example, Steven Spielberg – *The Goonies* (Richard Donner, US, 1985), *Gremlins* (Joe Dante, US, 1984); Jerry Bruckheimer – *The Rock* (Michael Bay, US, 1994), *Con Air* (Simon West, US, 1997).

- Screenwriter(s):

While few screenwriters have achieved lasting recognition among the general film audience, the large amounts of money that production companies are willing to pay to secure 'good' scripts suggest that the industry regards the script as a key element of a successful film.

- Cinematographer:

Like the screenwriter, few cinematographers have gained recognition among the wider audience. Nevertheless, they play a key role in designing and implementing the 'look' or visual style of a film, through their coordination and leadership of camera and lighting teams.

- Star:

As one of the key selling points of a film, it could be argued that many films exist as vehicles to sustain or adapt a pre-existing star image. As such, it would be possible to identify the star as the driving force of a particular film's identity.

Critics and academics have used the concept of film authorship to draw together groups of films from a single author or *auteur* (the term derives from French critics of the 1960s who were the first to engage seriously with this debate) in order to study how they reveal common characteristics and themes. The approach tends to draw distinctions between directors who are skilled or talented enough to be able to demonstrate individual engagement (the auteur) and those directors who merely competently carry out the task of constructing a film text (the *metteur en scène*). This way of thinking implies an opposite approach to genre study where the emphasis rests on the institutional and cultural background to film production, rather than on individual sensibilities.

In the classroom

Set up a group balloon debate, centred on the 'authorship' of a film you are studying. Students can take on the role of writer, director, star or any other creative personnel and must argue for the validity of their input into the film's production. The rest of the class have the chance to ask them questions about their role and then vote one person 'out' of the debate in each round. The winner – the author of the film – will remain at the end.

Key books

Nathan Abrams, Ian Bell, Jan Udris *Studying Film*, Hodder Arnold, 2001
Warren Buckland *Teach Yourself Film Studies*, Teach Yourself, 2003
John Ellis *Visible Fictions: Cinema, Television and Video,* Routledge, 1992
Susan Hayward *Cinema Studies: The Key Concepts* (Routledge Key Guides), Routledge, 2000
Mark Jancovich, Joanne Hollows (eds) *The Film Studies: A Reader*, Hodder Arnold, 2000
Jim Kitses *Horizons West: The Western from John Ford to Clint Eastwood* (BFI Film Classics*)*, BFI, 2004
Patrick Phillips *Understanding Film Texts*, BFI, 2000
Graham Roberts *Introducing Film*, Hodder Arnold, 2001
Thomas Schatz *Hollywood Genres: Formulas, Filmmaking, and the Studio System*, McGraw-Hill, 1981
Will Wright *Sixguns and Society: A Structural Study of the Western*, UOC Press, 1977

Websites

<www.learner.org/exhibits/cinema> a very engaging introduction to the craft of filmmaking suitable for GCSE students.
<www.academicinfo.net/film.html> an extensive gateway and directory of online resources on film, cinema and TV.

2 | The Hollywood film industry

In many ways, it seems a little pointless to study a film industry which is in essence the best-known film production culture in most of the Western world. However, it is precisely this familiarity which often prevents students from grasping the fact that the Hollywood approach is not the only system of filmmaking available. The tendency to see the classic Hollywood style as 'natural' and unchallengeable will often lead students to dismiss work from other cultures or other aesthetic sensibilities as inferior or unwatchable. Some understanding of the way in which the US film industry grew into its present state, then, allows students to begin to make important connections between the historical, economic and artistic factors which influenced the formation of this style.

Timeline

1895   Auguste and Louis Lumière patent the *cinématographe*, an early camera and projector system, capable of showing an image that could be viewed by a large number of people.

After first public screening is held in the basement of a Paris café, the *Salon Indien*. Most of the films were documentary shorts on everyday subjects such as *The Arrival of a Train* and *Workers Leaving the Lumière Factory*, along with some basic narrative subjects such as *The Gardener Watered*.

1899   George Méliès becomes the first filmmaker to construct a narrative from a number of scenes in his film *Cinderella*. Later, Méliès would become more famous for the development of trick photography and visual effects such as stop-motion, matte photography and multiple exposures in films such as *A Voyage to the Moon* (France, 1902).

1903   Edwin S Porter, chief of production at Edison Studios in New York shifts the studio's pictures towards narrative forms, most famously in *The Great Train Robbery*, a Western which exploited new techniques such as multiple camera positions and cross-cutting.

1905   The first specialist venue for viewing film – a nickelodeon – opens in Pittsburgh.

1908   As a result of an early studio cartel in New York, many independents move their operation across the country. The first filmmakers arrive in Los Angeles, attracted by the favourable climate, variety of locations and cheap labour.

The Birth of a Nation

1910   Intertitles begin to appear in films to communicate dialogue.

1911   Filmmakers start to insert credits at the start of their pictures.

1911   Two parts of D W Griffith's *Enoch Arden* are exhibited together, creating the first two-reel feature to be shown in public. Until this point, films tended to be one-reel affairs, lasting 10–12 minutes.

1914   The start of World War I interrupts film production across Europe, allowing American motion pictures to gain a dominant hold in worldwide markets.

1914   Winsor McCay's *Gertie the Dinosaur* becomes the first cartoon star.

1915   The premiere of Griffith's *The Birth of a Nation*, a three-hour Civil War-based epic which marked the arrival of the feature film structure still used by Hollywood – narrative complexity, naturalistic acting, expressive close-ups and so on.

1922   Robert Flaherty's *Nanook of the North* is released as the first non-fiction feature film.

1922	The Motion Picture Association of America (MPAA) is formed, run by William H Hays, to ensure that standards of taste and decency are maintained in Hollywood's products.
1924	Cinemas begin to show feature programmes, with more than one film at a time.
1927	Warner Bros., in association with Western Electric, develops a synchronised sound system for films, which debuts most famously in *The Jazz Singer* (Alan Crossland, US).
1930	Pressure from lobby groups, particularly the Catholic Church, leads to the adoption of the Production or Hays Code by the MPAA.
1933	The Payne Fund Studies conclude that films have a direct influence on the behaviour of young audiences.
1934	All films are required to have a certificate of approval from the Hays Office before release.
1937	Walt Disney's *Snow White and the Seven Dwarfs* is released in the US as the first feature-length cartoon. (Lotte Reiniger's *The Adventures of Prince Achmed* (Germany, 1926) was actually the first feature-length animation.)
1940	For the first time, agents working outside the studios receive a proportion of profits for helping to assemble talent and stories for production.
1944	Olivia De Havilland successfully sues Warner Bros. over a contract dispute. The ruling begins to weaken the powers of studios to hold actors to long-term contracts.
1945	The House of Un-American Activities (HUAC) is created as a permanent congressional committee to investigate subversive activity and evidence of communism in American life.
1947	The HUAC subpoenas 41 Hollywood witnesses in an investigation of communist influence in the film industry. Ten people are charged with contempt and arrested as a result of failing to co-operate. Eighty-four further personnel are blacklisted for supporting the Hollywood Ten.
1948	The Supreme Court's Paramount Decree ends the majors' monopoly of the film industry by forcing them to divest their cinema chains and making distribution practices such as block-booking and blind-buying illegal.
1950	Hollywood begins to develop strategies to compete with the threat of television. More colour films are released, widescreen formats are introduced, and various gimmicks are trialled, such as 3D films.

| 1952 | James Stewart becomes one of the first stars to sign an independent, profit-percentage deal, masterminded by his agent Lew Wasserman of talent agency MCA. It signals the studios' recognition of the power of stars to sell films. |

1952   James Stewart becomes one of the first stars to sign an independent, profit-percentage deal, masterminded by his agent Lew Wasserman of talent agency MCA. It signals the studios' recognition of the power of stars to sell films.

1953   The studios' standard seven-year contract deals are replaced by single- or multi-picture contracts.

1955   Studios begin to open up their film archives by building sales or rental agreements with TV broadcasters.

1956   United Artists withdraws its membership of the MPAA, following the Hays Office's refusal to grant approval for the film *The Man with the Golden Arm* (Otto Preminger, US, 1955). The subsequent success of the film forces the Production Code to become more liberal.

1966   Two films are granted exemptions from the MPAA Production Code because of their frank sexual content – *Who's Afraid of Virginia Woolf?* (Mike Nichols, US) and *Alfie* (Gilbert Lewis, UK).

1968   A voluntary rating system is introduced, classifying films according to their suitability for young audiences.

1969   A new wave of US independent filmmaking is signalled by the success of Dennis Hopper's *Easy Rider*.

1969   Sony introduce the home video recorder.

1973   Studios move film openings from midweek to Fridays in order to maximise profits from weekend filmgoers.

1994   Steven Spielberg, former Disney executive Jeffrey Katzenberg and music mogul David Geffen form a new studio – DreamWorks SKG.

1995   The first completely computer-generated film, *Toy Story* (John Lasseter, US), is released by Pixar and Disney.

1997   DVD is introduced as a home-film format.

2000 onwards   Hollywood is dominated by six transnational entertainment conglomerates – Disney, Fox, Sony, TimeWarner, Universal and Viacom. These studios no longer 'make' films but finance and distribute projects which are produced by scores of independent production companies on a freelance basis

The Hollywood studio system

Sometimes regarded as the Golden Age of Hollywood, the studio system established itself with the arrival of film sound in 1930 and over a 25-year period helped to consolidate the US as the dominant economic force in world cinema. The Hollywood film industry had developed into an oligopoly of eight companies:

- The Big Five (sometimes known as the majors):
  - Paramount;
  - MGM/Loew's;
  - 20th Century-Fox;
  - Warner Bros;
  - RKO.

- The Little Three (sometimes known as the minors):
  - Universal;
  - Columbia;
  - United Artists.

The Big Five companies were all vertically integrated, ie they owned production facilities or studio complexes, had a worldwide distribution network and owned their own chains of cinemas. The Little Three were smaller production and distribution outfits with few or no cinemas to their names.

There was also a profileration of independent production companies competing for audiences. Some of these independent producers, such as Samuel Goldwyn or David Selznick, were able to make films to rival those of the big studios in terms of scale and budget; however, most specialised in low-budget, small-scale films that ran as supporting features to the big studios' films.

The majors and the minors operated as film 'factories', employing large numbers of personnel – both creative and technical, actors and filmmakers – under contract in extensive studio facilities. Studios were run by central management teams, often dominated by individuals whose autocratic management style earned them the moniker of 'moguls'. Projects were planned in a roster style to make the most efficient use of each studio's skills and facilities and then delegated to producers, who were responsible for assembling the appropriate teams of stars, actors and crews.

Although the system is sometimes likened to a production line, in which films were 'churned out' to meet audience demand, this analogy misses the point that each film needed to be sufficiently unique or different from previous products to ensure that it was a success. As a result, the studios strove to achieve a process of regulated difference, in which films could be produced quickly and efficiently within the studio blueprint, while retaining some element of originality or novelty to offset the familiarity. In practice, many of the studios became associated with particular styles and genres as a consequence of their particular production practices. MGM was known for its flamboyant musicals and generally high production values, the relative wealth of the studio allowing a higher average budget than most of the other majors could afford; Warner Bros' gangster films, on the other hand, were characterised by a gritty and claustrophobic feel, partly as a result of the smaller sets and higher reliance on location filming, as the studio sold off assets to offset its massive pre-Depression debts.

In the classroom

In small groups, work out the advantages and disadvantages of working within an industrial-style filmmaking environment from the point of view of the following:

- actors;
- actresses;
- directors;
- screenwriters;
- producers;
- studio heads or moguls.

As a class, debate whether the environment is more or less conducive to good filmmaking than the organisation of Hollywood today (see below). See **Worksheet 15**.

Hollywood today

The big companies which survived the decline of the studio-system era gradually evolved into wings of massive media conglomerates. Today production companies 'acquire' films rather than make them. Although big-name stars and directors may still be contracted to a particular company, the majority of film personnel are now freelance and films tend to be sold as packages – with a script or concept, stars and a director as the most important ingredients.

The growth of subsidiary markets for film exhibition (TV, video, DVD) and the consequent potential for audiences to pay to watch the same film a number of times in different formats, encouraged many studios to begin investing heavily in 'event movies', often with star names, big budgets and an emphasis on scale or visual effects, to be released in cinemas at key times of the year (the summer and Christmas seasons, typically). The rise of multiplex cinemas allowed films to be released simultaneously on a large number of screens, moving the emphasis for a particular film's financial success onto its opening weekend and short-term

Student worksheets to support this guide are supplied at: **www.bfi.org.uk/tms**

profitability, rather than on a long run. Alternative revenue streams – merchandising, home-viewing formats – could be relied upon to treble a successful film's box-office takings or allow a poorly performing film to break even.

The video/DVD market has also been a lifeline for smaller, independent production companies. The demand for product and the exhibition opportunities that exist beyond the competitive environment of the multiplex have allowed many filmmakers to work outside the mainstream on low-budget, alternative projects. Cheap digital filmmaking technology has also encouraged experimentation from creative personnel no longer constrained by film's prohibitive production costs. When combined with the possibility of distributing films across high-speed internet connections, one could argue that filmmakers have never been in a better position to bypass institutional controls to ensure that their films reach an audience.

In the classroom

Draw up the plans for a marketing campaign based around a newly released film of your choice. Demonstrate how those plans could be easily adapted to extend the film's money-making potential through merchandising and home consumption on DVD. See **Worksheet 16**.

Hollywood and film language

In the early years of cinema, filmmakers, like any producers in a new medium, had to encourage audiences to learn to 'read' their products. The international nature of the Western film market in the early part of the 20th century ensured that film style was shared across cultural boundaries, as products moved easily between the US and Europe. Only after World War I, during which trade between the continents dried up, did the first vestiges of culturally specific film styles become evident. The following sections look at the development of the filmmaking system that has become known as the classic Hollywood style.

Narrative structure

The need to create film narratives that would be easily understood by audiences from a wide variety of backgrounds, with relatively little experience of watching films, led early filmmakers to aim for simplicity and clarity in their narratives. Narratives tended to be built around unambiguous chains of cause and effect at the heart of which were human agencies. Characters were psychologically motivated from an early point in cinema history, given a clearly defined set of character traits and set up with obvious goals to be attained. Even as narratives and characterisation became more sophisticated, these basic tenets held firm. The goal-driven protagonist comes into conflict with other characters or situations that threaten to prevent him or her attaining their desired ambition. The protagonist and the antagonist will be explained in terms of their dominant character traits and these traits will remain consistent, unless some causal event occurs to change them. Finally, the narrative will reach a conclusion in which all the major story strands will be resolved and any mysteries or unexplained events will be clarified; the majority of the time this state of closure will be complete and positive for the protagonist – a happy ending.

In the classroom

Ask students to develop film treatments, in which these basic Hollywood conventions do not apply. For example, a film concept in which there are no obvious protagonists, or one in which events occur without cause or explanation, or one in which there is no progression towards an ending with closure.

Look at the kinds of products they come up with and get them to consider whether these would be successful as cinema. Also ask them to investigate whether any 'real' films succeed without maintaining these 'rules'.

It is unlikely that any mainstream Hollywood products challenge the conventions, but you might use sequences from *Un Chien Andalou* to illustrate non-causal narrative, or from *The Battleship Potemkin* (Sergei Eisenstein, USSR, 1925) to show how stories can be told without the use of obvious protagonists.

Alternatively short films very often make an impact through the deliberate rupturing of cinematic conventions. Showing students examples such as *The Most Beautiful Man in the World* (Alicia Duffy, UK, 2002) or *About a Girl* (Brian Percival, UK, 2001) – both available on the BFI collection *Moving Shorts* (<www.bfi.org.uk/education/teaching/movingshorts>) – can help them to become aware of formal and stylistic choices outside of the commercial mainstream.

Camera and editing

Early Hollywood filmmakers understood that clarity of narrative was as dependent upon formal devices as it was upon content. Close-ups of actors, for example, could suggest their psychological state or emotions more clearly than a long shot; similarly editing could serve to create continuity in time and place to help audiences keep track of relationships in those dimensions.

It is worth noting that, in contrast to Hollywood cinema, which focused upon the ways in which camerawork and editing could function to create unambiguous narrative within a fluid and unobtrusive formal system (later known as the continuity system), filmmakers from other cultures were employing formal techniques to other ends. Soviet filmmakers were using editing to create psychological and political impact in their films, basing their work on the view that editing or montage could create dynamic tension. Thus time was deliberately stretched by cutting overlapping shots of an action in order to emphasise key moments, for example, the sailors' plate smashing, their first act of rebellion in *Potemkin*. On the other hand, jump-cutting could often reflect sudden or violent events on screen. Most famously, Soviet filmmakers frequently used editing to create thematic links between different sequences either diegetically or non-diegetically. For example, in Eisenstein's *Strike* (USSR, 1925), he cuts from an officer's fists banging down as he orders the massacre of a group of strikers to a butcher's hands as he kills a bull with a downward swing of his knife.

In Germany and France, filmmakers sought cinematic techniques which allowed them to parallel movements in other visual arts. German Expressionist cinema, exemplified in *Nosferatu* (F W Murnau, Germany, 1922) and *The Cabinet of Dr Caligari* (Robert Wiene, Germany, 1920), used highly stylised camerawork, sets and acting styles to express feelings and psychological truths in the most direct way possible. French Impressionism moved in the opposite direction, chasing naturalism in style, location shooting and 'realist' acting in order to create 'untheatrical' experiences to stimulate emotions in the viewer.

The Most Beautiful Man in the World

The arrival of sound

When Al Jolson announced to excited cinema audiences that 'You ain't heard nothing yet' in *The Jazz Singer*, it heralded a new era for global cinema. However, early sound technology created as many problems as opportunities for filmmakers and many felt that it was the beginning of the end for film as a creative medium. The first microphones tended to pick up every sound on set, including the noise of the camera's mechanism. As a result, cameras had to be placed in soundproof booths which drastically reduced their mobility. To compensate, many films of this era were shot with multiple cameras so that producers would still have a variety of shots from which to cut a single sequence together. In addition, sound could only be recorded 'as live' so that if music or sound effects were needed, they had to be played on set and carefully choreographed to the action. A key development in sound technology was the ability to record more than a single track, since this gave filmmakers the chance to record soundtrack music and sound effects after filming and coordinate these carefully with an edited version of the film.

The combination of multi-track, post-synchronised recording and advancing camera technology allowed movement back into Hollywood cinema in the 1930s. Dollies and cranes were introduced, facilitating tracking shots of increasing scale and complexity; crab dollies allowed cameras to move in any direction around the set. In addition, the ability of new camera lenses to compose frames in depth was exploited fully by filmmakers such as Orson Welles. This flexibility enabled filmmakers to compose intricate sequences, without the need for cutting, while retaining the basic tenets of Hollywood film style. The combination of camera and editing choices generated a huge palette with which filmmakers were able to create their narratives.

Colour and widescreen

Filmmakers of the silent era occasionally worked with colour film, by employing non-photographic processes such as hand stencilling film cells. The result was effective but labour-intensive and it was not until the introduction of three-strip Technicolor in the 1930s that colour filmmaking was considered viable by the studios. Even so, the decision to film in colour added around a third to a standard budget and was often only justified for historical sagas or fantasy films. As such, colour was often regarded as a signifier of the extraordinary or the exotic, rather than the index of realism it is seen as today (a well-known example would be the contrast that is achieved between Kansas and Oz in *The Wizard of Oz* (Victor Fleming, US, 1939), where the mundane existence of the former is connoted through the black-and-white footage and contrasted with the Technicolor fantasy of the Oz sequences).

The Wizard of Oz

Throughout the 1950s, the proportion of Hollywood films made in colour grew rapidly, as studios sought to differentiate their product from the small-screened black-and-white shows that were airing on television in a growing number of US living rooms. Competition with television was also largely responsible for the increased adoption of a variety of widescreen formats. Initially, there were fears that audiences wouldn't look at a widescreen in the 'right' way to follow action, leading to another period of static camera shots and slow editing as filmmakers attempted to convey information as effectively as possible in the new format. However, almost immediately, the principles that had supported the Hollywood style for the first half of the century were applied to widescreen composition, with directors choosing to build their narratives around the conventions of continuity editing and *mise en scène*, establishing a successful stylistic basis for decades to come.

The star system

During the studio-system era, stars were contracted to specific studios and their careers were mainly controlled and determined by the specific creative and economic demands of their employers. In the 1950s, the growth of talent agencies to represent the interests of actors led many stars to break free of the contract system and work on a freelance or short-term contract basis, often in

User name: **filmgcse@bfi.org.uk**   Password: **gc1603fi**

return for profit-linked financial rewards. The result was a shift in power towards the performers and their agents, one of the contributing factors in the decline of the studio system and the move towards a Hollywood model that continues to privilege stars as a key ingredient in a successful film package.

Although Hollywood is not the only example of a national film industry featuring a star system as an integral element in the way films are made and sold to audiences, it has been inextricably linked to the notions of stars and stardom since the early years of the 20th century. In order to understand the different ways in which the film industry, audience and academics think about the concept of stardom, it is worth considering how stars function in a number of dimensions.

■ Stars as economic commodities

Stars sell films. The Hollywood marketing machine invests heavily in the use of stars to raise awareness of their products, from on-set ENPs (Electronic News Packs) featuring interviews with stars to be distributed on the release of the film, through promotional tours, interviews and merchandising that are normally important contractual requirements.

Case studies of recently released films can demonstrate the range of promotional opportunities and the different ways that stars can be involved as part of a marketing campaign. Students could be encouraged to carry out their own research here to present to the class.

It is also important to note that the economic value of a star can be instrumental in getting a film made in the first place. Film scripts are frequently packaged with particular stars to attract investment and there are a number of examples where a star's interest in a script has allowed writers and directors access to financial resources that would not normally be available. For example, Johnny Depp's role in ensuring financing for Terry Gilliam's doomed *Don Quixote* project is illustrated very effectively in the documentary *Lost in La Mancha* (Keith Fulton and Luis Pepe, UK/US, 2002).

■ Stars as images or myths

Established film actors frequently carry with them the residue of previous roles, so that our perception of their performance is not a neutral one, but informed by our knowledge of their previous films and other characters that they have played. John Ellis draws a distinction between the performer and the star, saying that the star image is constructed not just out of previous roles, but also the meanings that surround a star in subsidiary media such as print products, the internet, TV, radio and so on. To some degree, stars will attempt to gain control of their image by ensuring that the material available about them sustains an existing image appropriately for their target audience, or adapts an image to sustain a long-term career strategy. This can be achieved relatively easily through their choice of film roles, but publicists and

PR expertise are often required to manage the role of newspapers, magazines or television in this process, with varying degrees of success.

Gledhill has written about the importance of the star 'body' in the construction of their image. Male stars such as Brad Pitt or Orlando Bloom signify attractive ideals of masculine health and virility through their good looks and muscular bodies; aging male stars (as long as they remain reasonably physically fit) are acceptable to audiences because they carry with them positive connotations of experience and sustainability. Female stars have a more ambiguous relationship with the audience as they grow older and only rarely sustain the same kind of star status as their physical appearance matures.

Richard Dyer (1997) perceives the star image as essentially paradoxical and unstable. Stars carry with them elements of familiarity, allowing audiences to identify and empathise with the image (they are like us, ordinary), while simultaneously revealing talents and qualities that are beyond the audience (they are different to us, extraordinary). In addition, stars exist as a semblance, simultaneously present through the various elements of their image which we perceive, but absent because the image is a construction and their presence, an illusion of light on celluloid.

■ Stars as cultural signifiers

Stars do not only stand for 'personal' identity groups of age or gender, but act to mediate wider social values between audiences and their cultures. The popularity of particular stars is often linked to wider issues of the cultural environment – the emergence of James Dean and Marlon Brando in the 1950s, for example, reflected the growing awareness of youth as a significant social grouping. Stars may also represent specific notions of national identity to their 'home' audience – a comparison of John Wayne as an icon of the US in the 1950s and Tom Cruise as a more contemporary signifier of 'Americanness' would reveal interesting differences in the ways in which US audiences see themselves. Alternatively, it is useful to look at the shift in a star's meanings as they are seen by foreign audiences; a study of Britishness as represented by Hugh Grant, Orlando Bloom and Ewan McGregor for American audiences would be productive here.

In the classroom

Create a portfolio of material based around a current film star of your choice. Through the range of materials and representations you have gathered, draw up a list of the key elements of the star image and the meanings which seem to be carried by this image. Are their any contradictions or tensions in the image that is projected? **Worksheet 17** will help students with this task.

Hollywood audiences

At the height of the studio-system era, 90 million Americans attended the cinema every week. Although films were targeted at different demographics – gangster pictures for male audiences, melodramas for females – most films were assured of a mass audience because of the habitual nature of cinemagoing. The large urban cinemas attracted family audiences by ensuring that attendance was part of an event, offering a programme of features, short films and newsreels, often interspersed with live entertainment or competitions.

When the introduction of television seemed to have captured the family audience in their domestic habitats, studios began to target other groups, particularly the youth market, in order to generate box office for their products. The abolition of the Hays Code in the 1960s allowed more challenging subject matter into film, alienating the family audience and creating clear distinctions between films aimed at mature audiences and those aimed at the younger end of the market. The success of 1970s' blockbusters such as *Jaws* (Steven Spielberg, US, 1975) and *Star Wars* accelerated the studios' pursuit of youth audiences to the point where, over succeeding decades, the 12–24-year-old target market became the key ingredient in determining how much money a film was likely to make and, therefore, how much money could be invested in it.

In the classroom

Use film-marketing materials to deduce how particular films are targeting this youth audience through:

- actors;
- narratives;
- visual styles;
- messages and values.

Do you perceive any difference in the target audiences?

A key consideration in any study of Hollywood audiences is the way in which the messages and values of the film are understood by non-American audiences. This issue is particularly pertinent in those marketplaces where US films are widespread – practically all of the English-speaking world as well as many countries where English is not the first language. In these circumstances, many commentators have noted the risk that the values communicated by these films are so widespread and reinforced so frequently that they usurp or mask native value systems, a process known as cultural imperialism. At its most obvious and crass, Hollywood film frequently sells the myth of America as the protector and saviour of global democracy. A viewing of *Independence Day* (Roland Emmerich, US, 1996), particularly the montage sequence of local populations praising the US military action against alien invaders, should make this point clearly. However, more subtle forms of 'Americanisation' can be found in many Hollywood products which privilege dominant US value systems in terms of social arenas such as the family, religion, law and order, governance and education.

Key books

David Bordwell, Janet Staiger *The Classical Hollywood Cinema: Film Style and Mode of Production to 1960*, Routledge, 1988
Richard Dyer, Paul McDonald *Stars*, BFI, 1997
Thomas Elsaesser, Warren Buckland *Studying Contemporary American Movies: A Guide to Film Analysis*, Hodder Arnold, 2002
Christine Gledhill *Stardom: Industry of Desire*, Routledge, 1991
Douglas Gomery *The Hollywood Studio System: A History*, BFI, 2005
Steve Neale, Murray Smith (eds) *Contemporary Hollywood Cinema*, Routledge, 1998
Thomas Schatz *The Genius of the System*, Faber & Faber, 1998

Websites

<www.filmsite.org> an excellent generic source with some great chronological genre essays.
<www.classicmovies.org> another site that makes Hollywood its focus in terms of content and judgment.
<www.pictureshowman.com> a site dedicated to the history and development of the Motion picture industry.

3 | Other film industries

The British film industry

After the first film screenings by the Lumière brothers in Paris, British filmmakers were quick to exploit the potential of this new medium. Although their first films were similar in subject matter to the novelty products common in France, British producers soon developed a number of approaches that were distinct from the competition. In particular, British filmmakers were associated with imaginative visuals and special effects. One of the most well-known early producers, Cecil Hepworth, used stop-motion photography to create amusing fantasy narratives, such as *Explosion of a Motor Car* (in which a car blows up and a passing policeman stands by as body parts rain down on him!). The Brighton School were a small group of filmmakers based around the South coast. Their creative approach to *mise en scène* and editing was also influential in creating an early British cinema. In particular, they pioneered the use of cuts in close-up shots to allow audiences to see detail, a technique which was to form the basis of the continuity style that developed later.

Despite this early promise, British filmmakers struggled in competition with European and American rivals. The influx of products from France, Italy and the US had already had a major impact on British cinema by the start of the World War I in 1914; the conflict inevitably disrupted film production across Europe so that, by the end of the war, almost 80 per cent of the films being shown in British cinemas were American. Hollywood domination of British cinemas has rarely let up since.

In the 1920s, the British government introduced a quota system to ensure that cinemas devoted a proportion of their screenings to British films. The system remained in place for a number of years, with rising quotas, so that, by 1937, a fifth of films shown in national cinemas had to be British. The demand for British films led to a sustained growth in the UK film industry (supported by American investment, to ensure that Hollywood studios were gaining some return from 'British' films) and a studio system of sorts was in place by the 1940s. A great number of smaller producers focused on the production of 'quota quickies', low-budget, swiftly made films, which enabled cinemas to meet their required quotas without the outlay required for bigger pictures. At the other end of the scale, Gaumont-British and BIP (British International Pictures) acted as majors, owning their own production facilities, distribution companies and cinema chains.

World War II then had an impact on the production of British films, but the stability of the studios allowed them to weather the situation more easily this time around, producing fewer films but maintaining the quality needed to continue attracting large audiences. Cinema was seen to have an important function in sustaining national morale and identity during the war and in the post-war period, as production companies such as Ealing Studios emerged with a succession of quirky comedies celebrating the values of community and patriotism in films such as *Passport to Pimlico* (Henry Cornelius, UK, 1949) and *The Lavender Hill Mob* (Charles Crichton, UK, 1951).

However, competition from the massive amount of Hollywood films and from the introduction of television in the 1950s finally took its toll on the major players and the British studios went into decline. In their place, smaller independent studios emerged, producing films aimed at younger, less family-orientated audiences. Hammer Films rose to prominence with a succession of gory, sensationalist horror films that were popular with both domestic and international audiences. Meanwhile, young British directors brought up in the tradition of documentary filmmaking in this country were producing fictional films characterised by their unflinching representation of the grimy realities of everyday life. Films such as *Room at the Top* (Jack Clayton, UK, 1959) and *Saturday Night and Sunday Morning* (Karel Reisz, UK, 1960), came to be known as 'kitchen-sink' dramas, examining working-class lives and cultures in ways in which British cinema had never previously dared. Although the trend was shortlived in cinema, its influence continued in the TV dramas of the day and the development of the serial fiction we now know as soap opera.

Saturday Night and Sunday Morning poster

Throughout the 1970s and 80s, lack of government support and competition from Hollywood blockbusters reduced British cinema to an all-time low in terms of the numbers of films produced. Despite some critical and commercial successes, the industry struggled to achieve a sustainable level of studio production and was kept afloat by a reliance on European co-production and the emergence of the heritage film as a profitable genre. Channel 4's film wing, Film 4, was a rare success story until its recent closure and other broadcasters such as the BBC have also invested in film production. However, only a small proportion of production companies has achieved any degree of sustained success. The future of British film may well lie in its ability to produce distinctive films that reflect the diversity of national values and cultures, rather than trying to compete in the mainstream market dominated by Hollywood. In recent years, breakout successes such as *Notting Hill* (Roger Michell, UK, 1999) and *The Full Monty* (Peter Cattaneo, UK, 1997) have performed strongly in both the domestic and US markets, but they remain the exception rather than the rule and rarely paved the way for future film accomplishment. The long-term future of the British film industry is still far from settled; the role of government support, Lottery funding and its relationship with Hollywood will be key elements in determining British cinema's path into the next decade.

Definitions of British film

There has always been some debate about what the term British cinema actually means. In the era of quotas, British films were defined as films made in Britain, with British casts and crews, yet many of these were financed by Hollywood. Today, only very low-budget films are likely to be funded entirely by British investors. Most products are made as the result of complicated co-production agreements with European or American producers and distributors, whose crew, and possibly cast, will often reflect the cosmopolitan nature of the investment. On the other hand, British production facilities, British crew and British actors are heavily in demand in a number of film-producing cultures, especially Hollywood.

Defining a British film, then, may be achieved through its content and its values rather than its institutional background. This kind of definition allows us to group together films as diverse as *A Room with a View* (James Ivory, UK, 1985) and *Trainspotting* (Danny Boyle, UK, 1996), or *Bend It Like Beckham* (Gurinder Chadha, UK, 2002) and *Shaun of the Dead* (Edgar Wright, UK, 2004). Each of these films presents us with a recognisably British environment and characters, while at some level defining or questioning those qualities which we understand as 'Britishness'. Indeed, in an era in which the boundaries of British nationality are constantly being challenged by regionalism and multiculturalism, it seems only appropriate that British film should reflect this variety and uncertainty.

In the classroom

Provide students with various DVD covers and credits from recent British films (or films with an obvious British influence). Ask them to draw up a list of the films that they believe are British and discuss the criteria which they used to make these decisions. See **Worksheet 18**.

Versions of Britishness

The following films pick up on some of the issues raised above and, in some ways, stand at opposite ends of the cultural spectrum. As such, they provide some indication of the range of themes that are generated by questions of Britishness.

Love Actually

The commercial success of *Love Actually* (Richard Curtis, UK, 2004) in both the UK and the US has been seen by many as an indication of the ability of British films to compete in a global market. Indeed the film seems to form a loose trilogy with two others that were also able to find international success – *Four Weddings and a Funeral* (Mike Newell, UK, 1994) and *Notting Hill* (Roger Mitchell, UK, 1999).

All three comedies were written by Richard Curtis (and he also directed *Love Actually*), star Hugh Grant as a charming but hapless romantic lead and construct their narratives around small networks of friends whose lives are developed through established social rituals – weddings, dinner parties and, strangely, press conferences. The idea of love as a key social determinant and the primacy of relationships as the basis for fulfilment and happiness are recurrent themes and all the films provide a key American character as a strategy for bringing the essential qualities of 'Britishness' into focus.

Love Actually can be defined as a British film through a number of criteria. All the key creative personnel – writer/director, star, producer and cinematographer – are British, as are the majority of the crew. The film was made by Working Title, a British production company. Most of the cast are familiar faces from British television and theatre and the narratives are generally played out in a recognisable reproduction of London at Christmas time. However, if the film's essential Britishness is not in question, the accuracy and relevancy of the national identity it reproduces does raise some interesting issues.

Love Actually

In many ways, the film borrows heavily from different strands of past British cinema. It uses many of the character types, situations and values of the theatrical traditions of British films – the middle-class dramas or comedies of manners such as Herbert Wilcox's *Spring in Park Lane* (UK, 1948) or *Maytime in Mayfair* (UK, 1949) – while often generating comedy from the misplaced social relationships and undermining of middle-class decorum evident in many of the Ealing comedies. The fact that both of these traditions reached their peak of popularity in the 1950s offers a clear indication of the conservative nature of the representations on offer. *Love Actually*, like its companion films, presents a version of nationality which appeals nostalgically to home audiences and stereotypically to international audiences.

Love Actually has many contemporary trappings. Hugh Grant's Prime Minister, despite being portrayed as apolitical, comes across as a younger version of Tony Blair, full of liberal idealism and with a social conscience; in turn, he has to deal with the bullying pomposity of an American president who combines aggression and moral ambiguity in a clear parody of George W Bush's presidential style. Various story strands take us into the world of sex scene body doubles, single-parent families, office affairs and, in a satirical swipe at the music industry, an ageing pop star on the comeback trail, following a serious heroin addiction.

However, the focus on white, middle-class characters, generally untroubled by the demands of work or finance, creates a view of society which is resolutely old-fashioned. In addition, the use of a Christmas setting (of course, accompanied by a comforting blanket of snow) further emphasises the stereotype of Britishness, seemingly lifted straight out of countless film versions of Dickens' stories. The sentimentality of the film's themes helps to underline the representations. Love wins out, despite the essential inability of most of the characters to express their feelings effectively, and in almost every case, the stereotype of British reserve is predictably shown to hide a deep well of emotions. The success of *Love Actually* in generating a mass audience both at home and abroad is due in large part to its ability to create a coherent and marketable version of British identity, despite its limited view of national culture. The final scenes of the film see the characters from most of the nine storylines converge at Heathrow Airport, a symbol of the conjunction of British and American values which pervades the film. As they reconcile and reunite at the arrival gates, the audience is also encouraged to feel it is better to arrive in this culture than to leave it.

Bullet Boy

Bullet Boy (Saul Dibb, UK, 2004) is based in the East End of London and follows the story of Ricky as he returns from a spell in prison determined to keep himself and his family (particularly his 12-year-old brother, Curtis) out of the cycle of violence and gun crime that blights his community. However, a minor confrontation over a broken wing mirror escalates into a series of reprisals between gangs that threatens to drag Ricky and his younger brother back into that culture. In many ways, this film stands at the opposite end of the filmmaking spectrum to the polished, commercial products that *Love Actually* seems to represent. The film was co-funded by BBC Films and the Film Council, with grants from the National Lottery and many key members of the production are British – star Ashley Walters, writer and director Saul Dibb, writer Catherine Johnson and producers Mark Booth and Ruth Caleb. The lack of established names in the cast and crew is one further indicator that the film is a relatively low-budget product.

Although the narrative structure of the film is similar to that of many American films – *Boyz N the Hood* (John Singleton, US, 1991), *American History X* (Tony Kaye, US, 1998) – few British films have attempted to portray urban teenage life in this way. The small budget involved precludes the film from trying to compete with the scale or spectacle of its US cousins (or indeed the 'star' power), so success is dependent upon the film's ability to create an experience that is different from these. This is achieved partly through the use of locations such as local estates and amenities familiar to British audiences, connoting the kind of claustrophobia and threat central to the film's narrative. The style of the film is also very different to the aesthetics adopted by mainstream Hollywood products. The documentary look in some way ties the film to its 1960s' predecessors – the kitchen-sink dramas – but also communicates the authenticity of the environment.

Bullet Boy

Dibb is a documentary-maker who came up with the idea for the film after seeing a headline in a local newspaper. His initial script was revised in collaboration with Johnson, a resident of Hackney who was working as the writer-in-residence at Holloway Prison. Much of the detail of the film's characterisation emerged from improvisation workshops run for the film's actors (some of whom were non-professionals, cast from the local area) and this added to the gritty, urban approach desired by the filmmakers. In addition, the casting of Ashley Walters in the lead role was an interesting choice, partly because he is best known to audiences as part of the London music collective So-Solid Crew, but also because he himself had spent time in prison for a firearms offence.

The film is mainly set in London's East End and peopled by members of its black population. However, this is not a film that is concerned with the ethnicity of the characters; rather, the narrative seems to stress that the issues being explored are strongly connected to the nature of the whole community and the claustrophobia of the urban setting. The film explicitly presents a contemporary view of Britishness that goes beyond narrow definitions of culture or ethnicity. The fact that it echoes many of the films which were part of the cycle of African-American dramas from the early 1990s suggests that *Bullet Boy* was made with an international audience in mind; however, it also provides a clear indication that filmmakers and film producers are beginning to acknowledge a wider range of appropriate subjects and topics for 21st-century British cinema.

In the classroom

Watch selected sequences from both of these films. Students should discuss the kinds of themes and values that are attached to 'Britishness' in the films. Which of the films presents the closest representations of their own experiences of Britain and why?

Key books

Justine Ashby, Andrew Higson (eds) *British Cinema: Past and Present*, Routledge, 2000
Robert Murphy (ed) *The British Cinema Book*, BFI, 2000
Jeffrey Richards, Anthony Aldgate *Best of British: Cinema and Society from 1930 to the Present*, Tauris, 1999
Anthony Slide *The Encyclopedia of British Film*, Brian McFarlane, Methuen, 2003

Websites

<www.britishcinemagreats.com> one of the largest internet guides to British films, cinema, films and the biographies of the best British actors and actresses.

<www.wickedlady.com/films> a site that considers the classic actors/directors and producers of 1930–1950s' British cinema.

<www.bfi.org.uk/nationallibrary/collections/16+/britishcontemp> a useful bibliographic study guide.

<www.screenonline.org.uk> the BFI's comprehensive resource site for British film.

The Japananese film industry

To many students, the films of US and UK cinema feel 'natural' and there is an assumption that they represent the only, or possibly the best, models of filmmaking. It is instructive to demonstrate to students that the forms and styles that they may take for granted are closely linked with the histories of film production and film consumption in these cultures. The fact that the US film industry dominates film production in many Western countries says more about the aggressive marketing and distribution of Hollywood studios in the 20th century than it does about any inherent quality or superiority of product.

Tokyo Story

A close study of the films of a different culture will enable the teacher to identify alternatives to the Hollywood model, while reinforcing the notion that film is as much a product of its era as of individual filmmakers. Although students may initially react against the introduction of unfamiliar approaches, with careful contextualisation and support as viewers, they will soon come to appreciate how rich and varied film languages from other parts of the world can be. Japanese cinema is an accessible and interesting example. Many students may have a working knowledge of contemporary Japanese filmmaking, either from a familiarity with exported genres such as anime or J-horror or from the influence of Japanese film on US films (*The Matrix*, *The Ring* (Nakata Hideo, Japan, 1998)) or other media such as games (particularly role-playing games (RPGs), the 'Final Fantasy' series for example).

Background

The introduction of film into Japanese culture was contemporaneous with film's birth into many Western cultures. However, this period was marked by Japan's transition from a hierarchical, feudal society to a militarised, modern socioeconomic state, heavily influenced by Western production methods. The dichotomies of the old and the new, East and West were ingrained in early 20th-century Japanese thinking as individuals struggled to reconcile the Japanese spirit with Western values. As might be expected, early cinema was equally affected by this dichotomy. Therefore, the technological innovation of the Lumière's *cinématographe* was balanced by the influence of traditional *kabuki* theatre in its presentation.

One of the most obvious manifestations of this was the presence of an interpreter/commentator or *benshi* who explained to the audience what they were seeing. The *benshi* became an integral part of the film-viewing process, as many of the exhibited films were American products, whose cultural frame of reference was alien to the Japanese audience. When films became longer and began to introduce narrative elements, story links were created by the *benshi*. The *benshi* filled time with rhetorical performances, drawing complex stories from simple images and guiding the audience towards moral conclusions. Frequently, *benshi* would steer narratives away from the original 'stories' in order to create their own tales and performance. Film audiences would be drawn to performances not by the subject matter of a film, but by a preference for a particular accompanying *benshi*.

Moreover, the presence of the *benshi* had an impact on the development of Japan's own film culture. Film was regarded as a development of theatre and many early films were recreations of theatrical scenes from *kabuki* or *shimpa* dramas. The *mise en scène* of Japanese cinema was heavily influenced by the concept of the theatre proscenium, so that there was an emphasis on extended long shots and careful composition of the set frame. Close-ups, pans and tilts were used sparingly and editing techniques such as cross-cutting or cutaways were rendered unnecessary by the *benshi*'s commentary. In the West, film style was developing towards forms of realism; however, in Japan, *kabuki* tradition led to a presentational style, which was not constrained by the demands of realism. Whereas Western cinema was developing a continuity style in which narrative progressed through conflict and confrontation (in terms of story structure, *mise en scène* and editing), Japanese film found an aesthetic based on harmony and similarity in order to tell its stories. Newsreel and documentary film became influential in Japan much later than in other film-consuming countries and their impact on the style of fiction cinema was less notable than in the US and Europe. As a result, Japanese audiences were much more open to the influence of presentational styles such as Expressionism in mainstream filmmaking than their US contemporaries.

Nevertheless, Japanese cinema was not immune to the impact of real life. Throughout the 1930s, government control of the film industry tightened and a more nationalistic regime became evident (and militaristic – the 1937 invasion of China was the first of a series of aggressive military tactics employed by General Hideki Tojo under the auspices of Emperor Hirohito). In 1939, the *Eihago* or Film Law was passed giving the government total control of the Japanese film industry. Japanese filmmakers were encouraged to produce films that reflected a national philosophy and foreign films were heavily censored: scenes of warfare or the negative effects of war back home were cut, as were inappropriate personal relations, eg kissing. The importance of social hierarchy was maintained and no material seeming to criticise or demean royalty was permitted. Japanese filmmakers were encouraged to celebrate the beauty of the family unit and the necessity of individual sacrifice for the good of the nation.

Following surrender to the Allied forces in World War II and the devastation wrought by US air raids and deployment of atomic weaponry, the Occupation regime was equally keen to control film output – filmmakers were to show the Japanese working towards peaceful reconstruction, Japanese military personnel rehabilitated in civilian life and a democratic emphasis on respect for personal rights. Allied damage to Japan was not to be shown, nor were members of the Occupying force. Despite these restrictions, it was evident that many filmmakers believed that they were better off than they had been under national government censorship and Japanese audiences once again looked to film as a way of redefining their national identity in the post-war era.

Several great directors emerged from the tensions of this period. Yasujiro Ozu's domestic dramas wed the formalist aesthetic traditions of *kabuki* to a modern preoccupation with family relations in a society trying to find equilibrium between tradition and modernity. In films such as *Early Summer* (1951), *Tokyo Story* (1953) and *Equinox Flower* (1958), Ozu examines the workings of family through the minutiae of domestic life. They are characterised by the director's sparse, restrained visual style and a reliance on long shots to distance the spectator from events so that they may be contemplated and considered. Key events may be alluded to but omitted from the narrative – in *Late Spring* (1949) the daughter's climatic wedding is not shown, only scenes of the father returning home alone and peeling a piece of fruit; Ozu uses the ellipsis to indicate that narrative events are less important than the truths they may reveal about the condition of his characters.

While Ozu's films focused on family and personal drama, other filmmakers painted on a broader social canvas. The *shakai-mono* or 'social-issue' film addressed issues inherent in the social and political organisation of Japan. Foremost among these were the works of Akira Kurosawa. Although Kurosawa tackled social commentary in a number of excellent contemporary dramas, he is best known by Western audiences for his period films – *jidai-geki* – such as *Rashomon* (1949), *Seven Samurai* (1954) and *Yojimbo* (1961). In *Seven Samurai*, a group of masterless samurai helps to protect a village besieged by bandits. The film explores the tensions between individual autonomy and one's duty towards the group or community in a complex way. The samurais' identity is defined by their duty to each other and to the villagers. It is evident that the samurai feel demeaned by their employment by the village, while the villagers resent their arrogance and superiority. At the end of the film, the bandits are destroyed and the villagers return to their farmlands, while the surviving samurai are left to wander once again. 'We have lost', comments their leader, Kambei: they no longer have purpose or status. The belief in the power of individuals to build groups is tempered by a scepticism that true equality and lasting values could ever emerge from the disparate needs of such a group. This was a potent message for a Japanese audience in the midst of reconstructing and reinventing their society following foreign occupation.

Kurosawa's use of the telephoto lens, multiple cameras and depth of focus in battle sequences created an intense and visceral experience of violence for his audiences as he attempted to develop the language of Japanese cinema to express his own ideas. Other directors were also concerned with innovation, developing the visual vocabulary to meet the needs of contemporary audiences. Suzuki Seijun's genre films of the 1950s and 60s did not have the emotional resonances of Ozu or Kurosawa's work, but found favour with younger audiences for their visual flair and imaginative *mise en scene*, as well as their amoral stance towards the characters' violent or sexual behaviour. In *Tokyo Drifter* (1966), a clichéd narrative of a criminal who is trying to go straight before being dragged back into a world of violent retribution, is given a fresh spin by the sudden changes of colour and lighting which accompany each act of violence. The protagonist's powder blue suit serves mainly to contrast with the blood that is liberally splashed during the final nightclub massacre.

Seven Samurai

Modern Japanese cinema

Until the 1960s, the Japanese film industry was structured around six major studios, along with a number of significant independent producers. However, the impact of television and the changing nature of film audiences in the 1970s and 1980s led (as in many countries) to bankruptcy, diversification and the collapse of the oligopoly. The changing nature of global cinema encouraged Japanese filmmakers to focus on indigenous genres, rather than competing directly with Hollywood product. In recent years, the success of some of these genres has reversed the cultural flow and a significant number of Japanese filmmakers have found that their talents and their films are in demand internationally. Kitano Takeshi made his name with a number of violent but lyrical crime or *yakuza* films such as *Sonatine* (1993), often examining the clash of individuality and humanity – *ninjo* – with the necessity of duty and responsibility – *giri*. The same themes are revisited in the UK/US/Japanese co-production, *Brother* (2003). Similarly a number of horror filmmakers have achieved international renown. The global success of *The Ring* (1998) opened the way for Nakata Hideo to move to Hollywood to direct the sequel to the remake of his original version (having already directed a Japanese sequel). Shinya Tsukamoto and Takashi Miike have also achieved acclaim with their more extreme cinema.

Perhaps the most influential genre of the new Japanese cinema has been one in which the fundamental ingredients characteristic of Japanese film from its beginnings – Eastern and Western, old and new, presentational and realist elements – have resurfaced as structuring principles: anime. The success of Otomo Katsuhiro's *Akira* (1988) paved the way for international recognition of a style of animation with a very different agenda to that of the Disney-style cartoon dominating Western cinema. Frequently tackling mature themes and content, anime is not a medium exclusively for young audiences. Anime characters are frequently *nihonjin-banare* (de-Japanised) with large round eyes and long bodies, yet the setting and themes are clearly linked to Japanese cultural concerns; surreal visual effects are commonplace, even when the animation strives for photorealistic effects, and cause-and-effect narratives are often eschewed in favour of expressionistic flow, built out of connection and association rather than linear logic. Studio Ghibli's *Spirited Away* (Hayao Miyazaki, 2001) exemplifies this 'dreamlike' quality of Japanese anime perfectly.

The following films can help students to explore some of the issues raised by the study of Japanese cinema. Both are accessible and interesting texts in their own right while engaging with some key themes of national identity and allowing students to consider questions of form and style. In addition, both films have been remade in Hollywood for US audiences, providing plenty of productive comparisons about the changes and compromises that have been necessary in the cross-cultural transformation.

Shall We Dance?

Superficially the narrative of *Shall We Dance?* (Masayuki Suo, Japan, 1996) seems to suggest a genre film in the mould of *Dirty Dancing* (Emile Ardolino, US, 1987) or *Billy Elliot* (Stephen Daldry, UK, 2000). Office worker Sugiyama escapes his mundane lifestyle by joining a ballroom dancing class; in the process he discovers unknown talent and learns to express himself through dance. *Shall We Dance?* certainly shares a redemptive 'feel-good' story structure with these films but much of the film's power derives from the way that it marries universal concerns with culturally specific issues. Sugiyama's opening voice-over explains that ballroom dancing is an anti-Japanese activity:

> In Japan, ballroom dancing is regarded with much suspicion. For a couple to embrace and dance in front of others is beyond embarrassing. A married couple would never think about going out arm in arm. Let alone dancing together.... To dance with someone other than one's partner would be misunderstood and prove more shameful.

Furthermore, in choosing to join the dance class, Sugiyama reverses traditional values by disrupting his social roles as husband/father, worker and citizen for individual gain. He is initially drawn to the classes by the beautiful and enigmatic

Mai, who he sees from his commuter train gazing wistfully from the window of the school, adding another level of possible transgression to his actions. His decision to attend the school marks a movement from a series of male-dominated, ordered environments – his office, home, commuter train – to a 'female' space in which the male characters' lives are thrown into turmoil by their interaction with teachers and fellow students.

Sugiyama's development as a dancer and as an individual is secured through his willingness to allow these two environments to coexist, and even merge. At one point he berates the workers in his office for mocking ballroom dancing as a pastime; his willingness to admit its influence on him is placed in contrast to his colleague Aoki, who secretly attends classes under an assumed identity, complete with wig and medallion. In many ways, Sugiyama represents modern Japan. He is a traditional figure, who finds his 'true' identity through the adoption of non-traditional characteristics. The popularity of the film with both Japanese and Western audiences suggests that this kind of compromise also functions at a cultural level. It is no accident that the film's title makes an intertextual link to the Hollywood musical, *The King and I* (Walter Lang, US, 1956), a film in which an Asian man (played by an American) is 'civilised' by the influence and art of a Western woman.

Shall We Dance?

Dark Water

Dark Water (Hideo Nakata, Japan, 2002) differs dramatically from *Shall We Dance?* in its tone and its representation of gender roles. The narrative focuses on Yoshimi, a single mother, forced to move into a rundown apartment block in order to provide some stability for her daughter, Ikuko, who is at the centre of a custody battle. The constantly leaking water from the apartment above is one of the numerous signs that the block is haunted by the ghost of a young girl whose intentions are unclear.

Nakata builds a chilling atmosphere through a dank *mise en scène* and a jolting soundtrack. His style is clearly influenced by horror filmmakers familiar to Western audiences, such as Robert Wise and Stanley Kubrick. However, his work is made distinctive through the assimilation of specifically Japanese cultural references. Water as a signifier of fear and dread has links with Japanese mythology, while the ghostly presence has theatrical ancestors in the form of Noh plays.

Nakata uses this tapestry of form and content to insert characters that differ significantly from the gender stereotypes in Hollywood horror cinema. *Dark Water* is strongly focused on female characters; men in the film are either exploitative (Yoshimi's ex-husband and the estate agent who sells her the apartment) or incompetent (the caretaker who manages the apartment block). However, Yoshimi is herself a flawed character, weak and paranoid, haunted by her childhood experiences of abandonment. She struggles to be a good mother. The pressures of single-parenthood are illustrated by the sequence in which Yoshimi tries to finish her office tasks while Ikuko waits alone for her in the school playground. Initially, it is unclear whether the spirit visions are manifestations of Yoshimi's anxiety attacks.

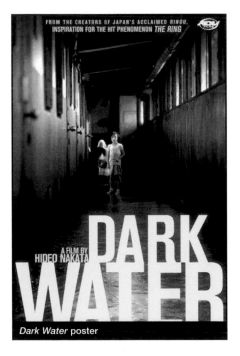

Dark Water poster

Images of lost and abandoned children litter the *mise en scène*. In this way, Nakata strongly links his representations of gender to the notion of the family. Indeed, the traditional family unit is conspicuous in its absence from the diegesis. Instead we are presented with acrimonious divorce proceedings, poor parents and vulnerable children. Nakata's society, signified by the decaying apartment block, appears to be disintegrating and the root cause is the decline of the family. In this light, Yoshimi's decision to sacrifice herself in order to save her daughter at the film's climax can be seen as an acknowledgement of the importance of the concept of motherhood beyond 'narrow' personal concerns.

Key books

Jay McRoy *Japanese Horror Cinema*, EUP, 2005
Donald Richie *A Hundred Years of Japanese Films: A Concise History*, Kodansha, 2005
Mark Schilling *Contemporary Japanese Film*, Weatherhill, 2000
Jasper Sharp, Tom Mes *The Midnight Eye Guide to New Japanese Film*, Stone Bridge Press, 2003
Isolde Standish *A New History of Japanese Cinema: A Century of Narrative Film*, Continuum, 2005

Websites

a site covering current developments and the latest insights into modern Japanese cinema – with archive features of past classics and masters.
<www.brightlightsfilm.com/japan.html> a rather highbrow journal on Japanese cinema but a good portal to wider genre links.
<www.greencine.com/static/primers/japan-60-1.jsp> a site that focuses on pre-1960s' material along a generic line.
<www.japanesestudies.org.uk/contents/filmreviews.html> a site that reviews modern Japanese cinema and also invites wider academic papers.
<pears.lib.ohio-state.edu/Markus/Welcome.html> a storehouse of information called the Kinema Club for academics and authors interested in Japanese cinema.

top right *Metropolis*

Case studies

One significant challenge in the teaching of film and of teaching English skills through film, is making the most appropriate and fruitful textual choices. While it's useful and interesting to encourage students to suggest films to study, sometimes it is best to be more totalitarian than democratic. Students can be highly knowledgeable in their film selections, but discussion can quickly disintegrate into subjective argument over 'voguish' preferences. One reason that often underpins a teacher's reluctance to make choices is a lack of confidence in their own grounding in film. These case studies are based on key film genres, each focused on a selection of two or three films, providing an introduction to the genre and an analysis of each film, with suggestions for classroom activities. We hope that these case studies provide a useful starting point for you while offering a template for study of other genres, such as musicals, Westerns or thrillers.

In our choices (sci-fi, action, teenage, comic book, Shakespeare, romantic comedy, adaptation and animation) we have tried to balance recognition of popular film genres with a selection of films that represent the breadth and versatility of these genres. The film selection is based both on what should be easily available and what may be unfamiliar enough to ensure that students' viewing is engaged and thoughtful.

At the start of each case study, there is a brief section intended to provide teachers with starting points for their GCSE Media Studies and media study in GSCE English. At the end of each case study, teaching tips and suggested classroom activities and discussion are designed to help the student focus more directly on the selected films and to inspire further study. The history of each genre is necessarily short and there is a wealth of reading material available on the internet and in libraries for students' research projects. Some suggested books and websites are listed at the end of each case study.

Each case study features a selection of online notes and worksheets. The 'Pause and Rewind' worksheet offers a list of suggested extracts for close textual analysis, featuring two key scenes from each film. These can also provide the starting point for speaking, listening, writing, reading and further research in Media or English.

1 | Future perfect? Sci-fi films

An examination of how present-day concerns manifest themselves in sci-fi dystopias.

Links to GCSE

- All GCSE Media specifications focus on a genre and it normally falls to the teacher to select the most appropriate. Sci-fi is effective in that it has cross-gender appeal and its history stretches from the early days of cinema itself. It is also a genre that has cross-fertilised many others. The dominance of special effects within current sci-fi is also an interesting development (see the BFI Film Links gateway for sci-fi and special effects).

- In GCSE English specifications, science fiction also features because of its literary lineage and the manner in which it reflects cultural, historical and social preoccupations.

- A good starting point for this Media/English consideration is the online Film Education resource, *An Introduction to Popular Genre*.

Part 3 | Case studies 1 Future perfect? Sci-fi films

78 Student worksheets to support this guide are supplied at: **www.bfi.org.uk/tms**

Like many genres, sci-fi is flexible, dynamic and amorphous, qualities that have consistently answered the needs of studios for big profits and reliable revenues, as well as serving audiences who want to question their anxieties and delve into their neuroses about the past, present and future. However, despite its ability to create a loyal fandom, critics often scorn it because of its 'lowbrow' appeal.

The ability to accommodate conflicting expectations is sci-fi's greatest strength and weakness. By being open to a range of different narratives, themes and influences, the genre can literally appear 'cosmic' in scale and classification. It could rightly claim to generate our modern mythologies and fairytales. However, we should not be awed by the dimensions of sci-fi. It is one of the most humane genres in that most films under its banner are preoccupied by the struggle between humanity and the inhumane, the familiar and the unfamiliar, the problems of the past and the perils and promise of the present and future. This not only governs the attitudes of the characters but also our responses as an audience. The sci-fi staples are films about insiders and outsiders, us and them. This is why successive generations of filmmakers have used it to address the concerns of their day and time. It is why the genre persists today in all its strange hybrids. There is no more universal fear than the fear of the enemy outside and within. This transcends race, gender and time. Sci-fi constantly reminds us not only of how fragile we are, but also of our great potential to respond and assert perhaps the central message of sci-fi: we are above all, human.

Background

The sci-fi genre is often about the successes and failures of science, rendered through a fantastical story. But sci-fi is not always about science. Sci-fi can be about anything, anywhere, at any time. While many sci-fi films are preoccupied with the wonder of science, it is often an arbitrary vehicle for the more important fiction of the text. This fiction can be based on a fantasy – on the impossible becoming possible (*Superman* – what if a man can fly?) – or on a cultural perspective in which some other world, distant in time or place, reflects back upon our time and place (*Star Wars* – in a galaxy far, far away).

This blend of the reality and the visionary is why sci-fi was one of the prototype genres in the genesis of cinema itself. Cinema as an art form emerged from early innovators' impulses towards the fantastic within the fairground arena. Filmmakers such as George Méliès (*A Voyage to the Moon*, France, 1902) began to set the foundations with his depiction of a bizarre, dreamily symbolic trip to the lunar surface. Fritz Lang then harnessed the sci-fi story to something more meaningful, a vision of a future industrialised and unequal society in *Metropolis* (Germany, 1927). Both these texts reveal that dual inclination in sci-fi to amaze and arouse the audience at a visceral and intellectual level. Sci-fi films after this point often strive to achieve either one or both of these. Through the paranoid Cold War sci-fi melodramas of the 1950s and the New Age, counterculture texts of the 1970s, sci-fi was as open as any text to the influences of one social or political viewpoint. However, the advent of the modern blockbuster in the form of *Star Wars*, and the manner in which it meshed so many of the key ingredients of successful modern sci-fi: action, spectacular effects, epic sweep and romance, created a sci-fi template that filmmakers in the 1980s and 1990s found difficult to diverge from. If they did (eg *Blade Runner* (Ridley Scott, US, 1982) or *Brazil* (Terry Gilliam, UK, 1984)) they often found themselves in conflict with the studios. Sci-fi films must not only attempt to reflect current social concerns (as in end-of-an-epoch texts such as *Armageddon* (Michael Bay, US, 1998)) but must work within generic constraints created by the success of previous texts. Perhaps it is appropriate that we begin our examination of the genre with a text that revels in this dilemma between same and different – the utterly familiar and the utterly strange world of *The Matrix*.

The Matrix

In the fast-changing, technologically competitive world of sci-fi and its arsenal of cutting-edge special effects, the original *Matrix* now seems an established classic. However, it is easy to forget the impact and almost immediate status this film gained, not only as a piece of entertainment but also as a cultural commodity and phenomenon. Not since *Stars Wars*

The Matrix

has one sci-fi film had such an effect on our global consciousness and the state of cinema production itself. Of course, we should not praise it for its technical innovation alone. Many sci-fi films promise and deliver some innovation and advancement in effects and spectacle. *The Matrix* was so successful because it was an amalgamation of audience concerns, pop-culture iconography, conspiracy theory, pseudo-religion and ancient myths all coated with a layer of escapist chic that made it irresistible. Its messages and values draw in so many

Part 3 | Case studies 1 Future perfect? Sci-fi films

80   Student worksheets to support this guide are supplied at: **www.bfi.org.uk/tms**

references, that many commentators have become preoccupied with deciphering this modern philosophy – called sci-phi.

However, as we are blinded by its techno glitz and intertextual glamour, it is easy to forget that the vast majority of people on the planet lack the basic technology to access films like *The Matrix*. It is not only obsessed with our obsession with technology, it is ignorant of technological facts. In other words, what are the messages and values behind a film that preaches a message of human unity against technology doing in a world where most people lack even the most rudimentary forms of electronic communication? With its preoccupation with the Western, white techno-literate perspective, is *The Matrix* racist?

The film begins with the most banal circumstances – a telephone conversation between the heroine, Trinity and the yet-to-be-revealed secondary villain. This telephone conversation spills over into an encounter, chase, escape, seduction, revelation, battle and rescue. The film ends with another telephone conversation when Neo, the now fully realised saviour of Matrix and Zion, challenges the computers to take the next step. In the intervening narrative, technology takes centre stage almost as an untitled character. Whether it is the now iconic streaming green text of *The Matrix*, the plug-in points implanted in the characters' heads, the mobile-phone portals into the Matrix or the creation of the flo-mo special effects, the film abounds in computer information, digital hardware, technological language and buzzwords.

The film is comfortable with these elements because it is comfortable with the audience's pre-knowledge and experience of these technologies. For a film in which computers and technology are perceived and portrayed as a potential threat, they are treated with an almost fetishistic reverence. In the world of *The Matrix*, weapons gleam, costumes shine, pavements are free of rubbish; Neo even manages to have a better haircut. The allure of this technology is best expressed when Cypher betrays his friends and Neo because the unreality of the Matrix is preferable to the supposed reality of the real world. However, the struggle to master this technology and therefore gain the mastery of *The Matrix* universe becomes the central conflict of the film. The question we may wish to ask is 'mastery by whom, for whom?' It appears to be no accident that Zion seems to boast a majority of multicultural non-white characters in direct correlation to the Matrix's majority of Western whites. We find out in *The Matrix Reloaded* (Andy and Larry Wachowski, US, 2003) that it is a place of drums, tribal dancing, extended families and meagre living. The film could be suggesting that certain cultures are less dependent on technology, and therefore freer. However, this presumption seems to have a stereotypical foundation. The characters who assist Neo are black – Tank, Dozer, the Oracle and Morpheus are all secondary and all dependent on the white Neo.

Therefore, *The Matrix* is not so much a racist film in that it disadvantages, mocks or neglects on a racial basis. But how would the film have been differently interpreted if Will Smith (an African-American and the Wachowski brothers' first choice for Neo) had accepted the role? Rather, it could be seen as a racist film in that its message of warning for the future is only applicable to a Western culture in the grip of technological obsession. Ironically, for a film that debates the perils of giving technology access to our lives and information, it forgets that many of its audiences have accessed the film and its ancillary texts through the technologies it inherently criticises, while many of its potential audiences remain such because they lack the basic facilities to watch, listen and read about a text such as *The Matrix*. The result is a film purporting to present us with a vision of the future but neglecting to show a genuine reflection on the problems of its times. This is a charge that could also be levelled at our next example.

The Terminator films

The unstoppable, unemotional, android assassin is a familiar character type in sci-fi. However, few of these characters have had the commercial success of the *Terminator* series let alone the effect of propelling the actor – Arnold Schwarzenegger – into A-list American film stardom and then into political power. Schwarzenegger is now so famous that his name is

The Terminator 3

recognised on the spell check in Microsoft Word. This synergy between star, character and narrative is something that we will explore further below.

Of course, when James Cameron wrote and directed the *The Terminator* (US, 1984), he could not have envisaged the growth of the franchise. The first *Terminator* film cost $6.4 million and grossed $78 million. The second film, *Terminator 2: Judgment Day* (David Cameron, US, 1991), cost $102 million and grossed $519 million. The third film, *Terminator 3: The Rise of the Machines* (Jonathan Mostow, Germany/US, 2003) cost $187 million and grossed $427million worldwide. That means that the overall profit of all three films (including merchandising) was in excess of $1 billion. This is an obvious illustration of the financial equations and monetary laws that govern the creation of a film and its potential exploitation as a franchise. The law of diminishing returns suggests that if a film is initially profitable then it can be relied upon for at least half that profit in each successive instalment. However, when a comparatively inexpensive artistic success, such as the first *Terminator* film, becomes a franchise with budgets, star pay and economic complexity and profits generated from merchandising, DVD sales and television rights, it can take on the proportions of some struggling national economies' GDP figures. Therefore, the

Student worksheets to support this guide are supplied at: **www.bfi.org.uk/tms**

creation of the third instalment may be more concerned with maximising the return on the good reputation of the first two films, than with offering any new interpretation or message of the post-apocalyptic world that may await us if we do not amend our ways. (All figures from <www.boxofficemojo.com/movies>.)

We are eased into the story of *Terminator 3: The Rise of the Machines* with a prologue that matches the epilogue of the previous film. One advantage of sci-fi films is that because they exist in the realm of the fantastic, the audience will tolerate lurches and changes in the scope of the narrative. At the end of *The Terminator,* Judgment Day was averted by the actions of Sarah Connor and her ability to annihilate the Terminator assassin. In *Terminator 2*, Judgment Day was averted by the actions of Sarah Connor, her young son John Connor and the assistance of a friendly Terminator. In *Terminator 3*, an older John Connor only delays Judgment Day with the help of an old girlfriend, a friendly Terminator, in battle with a new female Terminator. These developments show the same thematic concern of a film like *The Matrix* – the dominance of technology and the fragility of human decisions and therefore life. Key to *Terminator 3* is the redundancy of the Terminator technology and in some ways this film represents a lap of honour for Arnold Schwarzenegger as a redundant or no longer bankable star. It was his last big film (and therefore a pay cheque of $80 million) before he was elevated to political office. There is an obvious sentimentalism in his final demise and a hollowness to his infamously laconic catchphrase: 'I'll be back'. It is also indicative that Cameron declined to direct the third sequel. His status had increased with the commercial success of *Titanic* and he was reluctant to take what might appear a backward step. However, he was smart enough to retain the rights to the *Terminator* franchise.

Overall, *Terminator 3* represents a semi-successful end to a successful franchise. A franchise can start with a successful original film. It may then evolve and develop in terms of plot and character. However, much of a franchise's success depends on ensuring that all the original ingredients are included and revisited. The success of the first *Terminator* film spawned the sequels because there was an audience appetite for them and the institutional support to revisit the story to maximise profit. The advantage of sci-fi is that it can accommodate developments in character and plot. Behind this we also see that big-budget sci-fi films are increasingly becoming commodities and brands that are nurtured and protected as business ventures rather than artistic endeavours. Many film deals are only made on the basis that all players will commit to a sequel if the original proves to be a success.

The Day after Tomorrow

Roland Emmerich has a secure reputation as a director of sci-fi/action films that not only achieve commercial success, but tap into the Zeitgeist. *Independence Day* (US, 1996) reasserted American/Western constitutional values just as American pride overseas was being dented, while *Godzilla* (US, 1998) dealt with the effects of nuclear testing and mutation when the whole issue

The Day After Tomorrow

was newsworthy. However, we must ask the question – do sci-fi films reflect public and private anxieties to make deliberate political statements that in turn may influence the audience? Are these films now so popular that they are more effective vehicles for political influence than the parties themselves?

The Day after Tomorrow (US, 2004) is a classic 'what if?' film that takes an environmental issue (global warming) to its 'logical', exaggerated conclusion. The world begins to feel the effects of this phenomenon through city destruction, massive storms and freezing conditions resulting in the hero scientist attempting to rescue his stranded son. The film is packed with symbolism. There is an emotional 'freeze' between father and son. The son burns the books of the New York Public Library, suggesting that such knowledge is now irrelevant. However, the main issue is the almost propagandist preaching of the film and the way it warns and counsels the audience. This is implied in many of the film's set pieces. The Statue of Liberty is locked in ice, suggesting that the values it represents (liberty, fraternity, equality) are no longer active in society. The mass exodus of the American population into Mexico, reversing the stereotype of the migrant refugee, suggests that Western society will eventually be punished for its arrogant neglect of the Third World.

It is appropriate to see these as deliberate messages. Roland Emmerich is a registered Democrat. *The Day after Tomorrow* was released before the re-election campaign of George Bush. One of the key issues in this campaign was the President's refusal to sign the Kyoto protocols to halt the influence of global warming. However, like most propagandists, Emmerich has taken a popular genre (the disaster film) and adapted it to meet his ideological needs. This is apparent in the first section of the film when the hero is attempting to convince the people in power that disaster is looming. His concerns are repeatedly rejected on the grounds of political expediency.

The abiding image is the flooding and destruction of the New York cityscape. New York has come to represent the best and worst of American civilisation. The

Student worksheets to support this guide are supplied at: **www.bfi.org.uk/tms**

people on the ground appear to go about their business even as catastrophe is imminent. One telling scene sees a group of businessmen 'buy' their way onto a bus to protect themselves from the rain. The 'biblical' flood quickly punishes them for their selfishness and the only people who appear to survive are those who are seen as free from blame in this capitalist society (families, public servants, students and the homeless).

Teaching suggestions

Tips

Students often only want to watch films, not think about them. Use selective viewings as stimuli to encourage 'active' viewing. To facilitate this:

- use the time counter on your DVD/video player to set up the sequence beforehand;
- take advantage of the 'open' nature of sci-fi to create selection/placement tasks, asking students 'What makes a sci-fi film a sci-fi film?'
- look at the source material for sci-fi texts – compare the book version to the filmic one.

Worksheet 19 Pause and rewind has details of sequences from the films.

Activities and discussions for students:

- Mind map: **Worksheet 20** will help to trace the conventions of sci-fi. (The worksheet can be used for other genres.)
- Experience of sci-fi: views of or preferences? What are the differences between male and female responses to the genre?
- Compare the characters, Neo (*The Matrix*) and John Connor (*Terminator* films). How are they portrayed as 'saviours' of the world?
- How is *mise en scène* used to convince us that what we are seeing is 'real'?
- How does the media represent the future? Is it to be welcomed or feared?
- After considering several sci-fi films: Who is the real star of sci-fi – the actor, the director, the narrative or the special effects?
- How is technology portrayed in films like *The Matrix* and *The Terminator*? Is technology our friend or enemy?
- Design some (safe) sci-fi 'special effects' and shoot the results. How convincing do these look on screen? Why?
- Write a speech convincing a reluctant audience that the world is about to be invaded by aliens. (Read Orson Welles' famous broadcast to America for ideas.)
- Most museums have a science exhibition. Interview a specialist from the museum to find out the story behind a certain artefact or exhibit.

- The present and the future: Use **Worksheet 21** to take a theme – eg war, the environment, entertainment – and write about its manifestations in the present and in the future.
- A new world: Using **Worksheet 22** as a starting point, write about a personal dystopia or utopia.

Key books

Geoff King and Tanya Krzywinska *Science Fiction Cinema, from Outer Space to Cyberspace*, Cambridge University Press, 2002

Kim Newman *Science Fiction/Horror Reader: A Sight and Sound Reader*, BFI, 2001

Sean Redmond (ed) *Science Fiction Cinema: From Outer Space to Cyberspace*, Wallflower, 2004

J P Telotte *Science Fiction Film (Genres in American Cinema)*, Cambridge University Press, 1999

Websites

<www.filmsite.org/sci-fifilms.html> an excellent grounding in generic structure and key examples.

<en.wikipedia.org/wiki/Science_fiction_film> a free resource and especially good in establishing the links between cinematic and literary sci-fi.

<www.geocities.com/Hollywood/Lot/2976/SF_FilmResources.HTML> a very good central hub that acts as a gateway to other sci-fi related sites.

2 | Creating an impact: Action films

A look at how action-adventure sequences are constructed to involve audiences in the action.

Links to GCSE

- In the GCSE Media specifications, action films offer excellent examples for technical analysis and the construction of texts in how they create their effects on the audience.

- Within GSCE English specifications, action films are often used as provocative stimuli to discuss the representation of conflict, violence and male/female heroes.

▶▶

◄◄

■ A good starting point for thinking about this genre is a personal page by William Fulks, (<www.99.epinions.com>) listing his all time Top 20 action sequences, with enthusiastic descriptions of their effectiveness. From an English perspective, the Media Awareness Network (<www.media-awareness.ca>) is a provocative starting point in its desire to restrict the viewing of action films to a teenage audience.

Focus films

Superman: The Movie (Richard Donner, US, 1978) and *Superman Returns* (Bryan Singer, US, 2006)
GoldenEye (Martin Campbell, US, 1995)
The Lord of the Rings trilogy (Peter Jackson, US/NZ, 2001–3)

It is no accident that when a director wants to film any movement or sequence on camera, they shout, 'Action!'. A driving motivation in cinematic creation is to entertain through the presentation of extreme situations and energetic filmmaking. The action-film genre is a staple of global film production because its commercial performance is reliable. Every major studio annually releases a major action film as a way to guarantee revenue and offset the production risks of less popular films. The genre seems to be an important rung on the career ladder of many A-list Hollywood stars. Few leading actors have succeeded without this and it is often considered to be a litmus test of their box-office appeal.

Action films have tremendous crossover genre potential, and include hybrids such as adventure, sci-fi, thrillers, crime, fantasy, war or horror. Generally such films are commercially successful but do not garner critical praise. The genre itself is known for its high-concept, often ludicrous scenarios and setups, enhanced by heightened drama, an assault on the senses and a kinetic (and sometimes balletic) approach to violence. Plotlines are punctuated with stunts, extensive chase and fight scenes, rescues and escapes, and a non-stop determination to ensnare an audience and increase the sense of spectacle they will experience.

At a technical level, for an action film to be successful, all the elements of camera, editing, sound, *mise en scène* and special effects must combine to create an experience of unalloyed enjoyment. Action sequences are the best expression of this aspiration. The action sequence itself is an audiovisual, emotive experience that will attempt to overpower the audience with thrills, spills and kills. It is indicative that many action-film sequences are converted into virtual 'rollercoaster' rides. Critics have compared the effect of a well-made sequence to a 'ride' that challenges the audience to keep a grip, as the creators of the film attempt to throw them off with a series of increasingly impressive and extravagant climaxes – 'carrier waves' of action that literally carry the audience through the course of the narrative. These tense and involving situations build towards that ultimate moment of showdown and conquest when the hero faces and overcomes his greatest moment of peril at the hands of the villain.

Background

Action films are traditionally targeted at male audiences. The film genre developed out of a loose integration of the war films of the 1940s and 1950s, the disaster films of the 1960s and 70s and the Bond franchise. It expanded in the 1980s and 1990s with the development of new special-effects techniques and CGI (computer generated imagery) in response to competition from sci-fi blockbusters and the audience's appetite for ever-increasing levels of stimulation. One of the inherent dilemmas of the action genre is that each new film must try to outdo the previous one in terms of scale and impact. This means that audiences expect constant improvements in look and style that, if not delivered, can undermine a film's global competitive success.

The basis of the action narrative is often a simple portrayal of a 'good' protagonist versus a 'bad' antagonist, a conflict that represents a battle between morality and immorality. The story will focus on the physical and emotional journey of the hero. There is generally a sense of grievance and/or a search for justice. Critics have also commented on how most action heroes inhabit a dualism or a place in two worlds, and the conflict often derives from the clash between the competing needs of these rival worlds. For example, in *True Lies* (James Cameron, US, 1994) the hero is propelled into action because his wife discovers his spy identity. This clash between duty and domestic commitments is symbolic of the hero's internal and external struggle to return his life to normal after the disruption caused by the villain or other disruptive forces.

The hero may take many forms (however, bar some notable female exceptions to broaden the appeal of the genre, they are generally male) but a regular motif is that the hero must overcome a set of testing obstacles from which they will emerge changed and victorious, usually because of their resourcefulness. At some point they may lose confidence and abandon their quest, before rediscovering their purpose. During his journey, the hero may have a helper or buddy who provides comic relief to the action, with bouts of verbal sparring, throwaway one-liners and catchphrases. This often leaves these films open to accusations of flippancy in their depiction of violence and there is a 'staged' quality to action films that has become more apparent as films and video games have merged and influenced each other's style and construction.

Action films must strike a balance between realism and escapism, especially in their depiction of screen violence. People die in horrendous and melodramatic ways. Critics suggest that this is why audiences are unaffected by the violence because they understand that it is artificially inflated and hyper-real. These films must be believable and unbelievable at the same time, so that the audience is surprised but not shocked, unsettled but not repulsed.

At the simplest level, irrespective of how it is achieved, the main objective of the action film is to entertain, involve and preoccupy an audience for the duration of the film. It is designed for immediate satisfaction rather than ongoing reflection. As such, the genre has been criticised for being vacuous, failing not reflect wider social, racial or historical issues, or using facts or events relating to these issues in a fictionalised, hyperbolic way to be entertaining. For example, in recent years the action genre has been affected by the events of 11 September 2001, as Hollywood studios responded by altering films and rescheduling releases, or rushing out films that reflect a new sense of national defensiveness.

However, despite being dominated by what some might consider a cynical commercialism, action films are so beloved by institutions and audiences, it is unlikely that they will disappear from our screens. In the future, directors will continue to shout 'Action!' as a word that signals and suggests the impact and spectacle of cinema.

Superman and *Superman Returns*

In the pantheon of action films, *Superman: the Movie* (Richard Donner, UK, 1978) sits at the top of the list, in terms of cultural persistence, popularity and recognition. The 'iconic' nature of Superman is also linked to the values the character represents and embodies.

Superman

It is useful to reflect on the fact that Superman is an immigrant, an alien, seeking security away from his home world, which was destroyed by political inaction. This, of course, reflects the era of Superman's creation between two world wars, at a time of great migration. This is also perhaps the first reason Superman 'adopts' the values of his new homeland. Another reason is that

Superman is raised within the heartland of America, a farming community, distant from the cynicism of Metropolis. Smallville and the Kent family accept Kal-el, the outsider, and turn him into Clark Kent, the mild-mannered youth, striving to come to terms with his history and his growing awareness of his difference from others.

It is clear from his choice of costume and its colour that Superman wants to represent the 'red, white and blue' of the American flag and therefore American values. This is also reflected in the alter ego that Superman assumes. Clark Kent is a journalist interested only in truth, idealism and living his life in a clean-cut and conservative manner. Superman's allegiance to American values is also expressed in his actions. In *Superman 2* (Richard Lester, US, 1980), the hero defends his new world from criminals from his homeland. At the end, we see Superman replace the destroyed roof of the White House and carry the flag proudly. He also makes a promise to the President that he will always be there. In *Superman 4* (Sidnie J. Furie, US, 1987), we see him intervening on a global scale and ridding the world of nuclear weaponry, only to face the emergence of a vaguely Russian nemesis.

Although these narrative strands are engaging and entertaining, the message is plain: American values will always exist, dominate and survive. This is also expressed in the nature of Superman himself. He symbolises the unquestionably great might and strength of the American nation and its 'vision' of spreading these values globally.

In the 're-imagining' of *Superman Returns*, we lose much of the jingoism and nationalistic swagger of the original. This is very much a 'chastened' version of the Superman mythology in a post-September 11th context. The rise of 'alternative' heroes and unconventional figures in the action universe could be interpreted as a backlash against blatant patriotism and global domineering. One important recent development is that the *Superman* 'comic' brand has taken on an international direction. There are now Indian, Russian and South American versions of Superman, sensitive to local customs but still promoting the 'American' way. This perhaps shows that the creators of Superman are responsive to the fact that he has become too closely identifiable with American values. However, the literal and cinematic arrival of a 'new' Superman is still heralded by that most reliable of audience hooks – the action sequence. Even in this 'adaptation' of the original, there is a persistent reliance on those moments that thrill through their evocation of mayhem and the promise of imminent chaos that can only be contained or averted by an invented hero figure.

This quality is also abundantly present in that most iconic of action heroes – James Bond.

GoldenEye

James Bond is a constant within the action genre. As an action hero, he typifies the self-possessed character, always ready to employ humour or violence to disarm his enemies and seduce his female stars. As the international spy, he is core to the chaos that often ensues from his actions. The success of the *Bond* franchise is in part attributable to successful casting and focused attempts by the Broccoli family (the

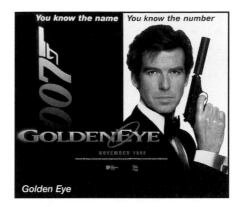

Golden Eye

owners of the licence) to ensure that each reincarnation of the character bears some resemblance to the previous players (Dalton, Moore, Lazenby, Connery) with enough difference to appeal to a fresh generation. If successful, it means that the established audience sees enough of the 'old' Bond in the new one – it is no accident that Brosnan with his Celtic roots, charming looks and quick temper appears to be an amalgam of the previous Bonds. Each new audience feels attached to 'their' Bond, who then becomes 'their' favourite.

This dilemma of appearing the same but changed is apparent in the opening sequence of *GoldenEye*, the film which introduces Pierce Brosnan as the 'new' Bond. Initially, his identity is concealed through a variety of angles. This not only builds anticipation but lets the audience take in the spectacle of the location (a massive dam supposedly in rogue Russian hands). It also allows the stunt actor to complete one of the spectacular acts that these opening sequences are renowned for, in this case a leap of faith into the cavern with the help of a retractable bungee rope. In addition to spy technology and physical danger, the focus on the hero and our identification with him is developed through close-ups on his eyes and black costume. However, it is only when we begin to see and hear Bond react to danger with his customary insouciance that we feel totally at ease with the new portrayal.

Bond then meets with his fellow spy, 006. As they set detonators, we see them experiencing an onslaught from Russian troops. The speed and ease with which 007 kills and dispenses with the enemy gratifies audience expectations of mass mayhem without exposing them to the reality of death. It is only when 006 is captured and killed after he urges James to 'finish the job', that we see an emotional reaction from Bond. However, this is fleeting as the need to complete his mission and escape to fight another day becomes paramount. In the following sequence, we see Bond make his escape. The instantly recognisable theme music reflects Bond's predicament and builds our anticipation of his impressive getaway.

We see Bond running and attempting to 'catch' a departing plane. We forgive the ludicrous nature of this escape only because it is such a challenge for Bond. He must dodge the enemy as he pursues the plane on a motorbike. But he apparently has nowhere to go and the enemy stop their pursuit. Again, epitomising the character and the genre, Bond faces an impossible trap that requires his special brand of escapology, along with his ability to bend the laws of physics. We see the plane launch over a precipice, while Bond, in free-fall, catches the plane, climbs inside and sits himself at the controls. He must then escape a death plunge to the chasm below. As the plane dips below the horizon and then climbs triumphantly over the now exploding enemy base, the credits and song are introduced to signal the beginning of the film. At this point the sequence has achieved its aim to introduce the character and the main narrative. However, it is important to note that the sequence only works because of the 'magnetic' nature of Bond. He is the cause of the mêlée at the centre of it, and therefore is a perfect example of why we watch action films – to see characters face and evade peril.

The Lord of the Rings

A feature which takes the action adventure into a different realm is the growing tendency to combine real and unreal (CGI) footage. Of course, other technologies have achieved this is in the past. The use of matte shots to suggest backgrounds, back projection to suggest movement and stop-motion to create monsters are all early

The Lord of the Rings

precursors of this style. However, only in recent years have we begun to witness the flawless melding of real and unreal action, aimed at making the unreal world of imagined places real to us. This is particularly true of the escapist, fantasy-action trilogy, the cinematic adaptation of Tolkien's book, *The Lord of the Rings*. *The Lord of the Rings: The Fellowship of the Ring* (Peter Jackson, US/NZ, 2001) evidences the seamless nature of this coupling. A prime example is when the Fellowship is at its lowest point. In the Halls of the Dwarf Kings, the Fellowship is stunned to realise that the standing army of dwarf-miners has been decimated. As they quietly contemplate their next move, the inquisitive nuisance that is Pippin accidentally tips an armoured corpse into a well. The resulting racket is the heralding call for an Orc army to attempt to enter the small, funeral chamber that the Fellowship has retreated to. Up to this point, all action has taken place in real time, with real actors and in the style of cross-cutting that is familiar to action audiences. The hobbits are portrayed through the use of high angles and diminutive actors and the Orc enemy is created with make-up and prosthetic masks.

However, the Orc army has a 'cave troll', a 16-foot monster which needs to be portrayed and rendered in a different manner, creating a practical dilemma for the filmmakers. To shoot combined footage requires a level of communication and co-operation between all players. The cave troll is a CGI character added in post-production. This is why many of the shots in the sequence have a simple foreground/background appearance. This is the CGI animators' canvas, allowing them to 'paint' the troll into the background in post-production.

The process of building the sequence is more akin to choreography than standard filmmaking, in that every element must connect to create the illusion of reality. This sequence is a battle and therefore requires interaction between friend and foe. The reactions and emotional responses of the actors are the first element in this approximation of reality. Confronted with nothing but empty space on set, they must appear shocked and terrified.

Another element that helps to bridge the real and unreal is the use of animatronics. These large-scale, electronic puppets often appear in partial shots, for example, when we see the arm of the cave troll or, in the final shot, the cave troll's dead mass when it has been killed.

The filmmakers employ other effects to enhance the action. When the cave troll hits the walls and floor with his hammer, we hear small explosions. In the troll's facial expressions, mouth movements and skin texture and scale, the character is never less than terrifying and threatening. This impressive sequence is actually upstaged in the next sequence with Baldrock, a flaming fire demon showing that the only true limit to this technology is the imagination of the filmmakers.

All action sequences may one day be rendered by computer. Films like *Sky Captain and the World of Tomorrow* (Kerry Conran, US, 2004), shot wholly in blue-screened sound stages, show this growing inclination and strange reversal. In the past, much of an action film's budget was expended on special effects. A film's budget can be significantly reduced by the use of CGI. However, audiences are drawn to a film because of the characters' emotional journeys. We are only responsive to their problems if we feel that they ring true to some extent.

Teaching suggestions

Tips

As action films dominate cinema screens, they also dominate students' interests. They may be excited by a chance to watch their favourite films for free in school, but the educational purpose needs to be clear. The support site for teachers <www.tes.co.uk> run by the *Times Educational Supplement*, features advice on how to present films within an educational context. In connecting with learning objectives action films can help students:

- consider the portrayal of heroism and villainy on film and the ideological messages that accompany these representations. The site <www.teachit.co.uk> offers free materials and schemes of work related to this topic;
- compare fictionalised heroes and villains with real historical ones in biopics;
- expand their knowledge of the action-film genre by viewing classics, comparing for example, *Ben-Hur* (William Wyler, UK, 1959) and *The Gladiator* (Edward Sedgewick, US, 1938);
- develop their understanding of the genre structure by looking at opening, mid- and end sequences.

See **Worksheet 23 Pause and rewind** for details of sequences from the films which have been successfully used in class.

Activities and discussions for students:

- Compare heroes: James Bond is the embodiment of cool sophistication; Frodo (The *Lord of The Rings*) is a hobbit with long ears and big feet. What makes a hero? See **Worksheet 24**.
- Action films are about action, movement and drama. How is editing used to make the action more exciting and dramatic?
- Heroes are often white, American males. How do action films represent villainy? Who is the enemy in these films and are they represented fairly? Has this changed in recent action films?
- Action films that are successful often become a franchise or trilogy. How do these franchises keep the characters fresh and interesting to the audience over such a long period? Look for example at the *Die Hard* (US, 1988–2007) or *Indiana Jones* (US, 1981–2008) franchise.
- Action films are often about chases. Plan a sequence where the hero and villain are involved in a chase, making it as tense and dramatic as possible.
- Every action film has a climactic ending. Use **Worksheet 25** to explore how one such ending achieves its effects.
- 'My Precious', says Gollum, expressing his feelings for the magical ring. Write about something that is precious.
- Some action novels now are written as if they are film scripts. Read extracts from the recent *Harry Potter* books and compare them to the films. Are books now being written more often to suit the needs of cinema, rather than the reader?

Key books

Jose Arroyo (ed) *Action/Spectacle Cinema: A Sight and Sound Reader*, BFI, 2000
Geoff King *Spectacular Narratives: Hollywood in the Age of the Blockbuster*, Taurus, 2001

Yvonne Tasker *Spectacular Bodies: Gender, Genre and the Action Cinema*, Routledge, 1993

Yvonne Tasker *The Action and Adventure Cinema*, Routledge, 2004

Websites

< www.filmsite.org/actionfilms.html> a clear and detailed coverage of the Action genre.

<en.wikipedia.org/wiki/Action_movie > a brief coverage but excellent to explore the links to famous action stars.

<www.everything2.com/index.pl?node_id=1687230> 'Girls Kick Ass: A Feminist Critique of the New Action Heroine and the Male Gaze': a complex, polemical but useful article.

3 | **Watch yourself: Teen films**

An examination of the relationship between teenage audiences and screen representations of teenagers.

Links to GCSE

- Both English and Media GCSE specifications feature studies of the teenage mindset and the representation of youth and teenage issues, in particular how the 'rite of passage' into adulthood is handled and portrayed and how this is interpreted by children and adults. Students might have strong views on this issue themselves, which can be used as a starting point for this topic. In an interesting article, 'Pop, speed and the MTV aesthetic in recent teen films' (<www.nottingham.ac.uk/film/journal/articles/pop-speed-and-mtv.htm>), Kay Dickinson suggests that current teen films are being deliberately altered in terms of pace, rhythm and content to match a misguided adult belief that this is all that the teen mind craves and can tolerate with its limited attention span. This serves as a provocative point for discussion about who creates teenage 'texts' and how often teenagers have the opportunity to represent themselves in their own work.

- For English specifications, the media education website (<www.mediaed.org.uk/forum>) has an excellent discussion board that encourages input from teenagers, giving them a platform for their views.

- From a Media Studies perspective, organisations such as First Light (<www.firstlightmovies.com>) provide support and funding for young people's filmmaking.

Mean Girls (Mark S Waters, US, 2004)
Donnie Darko (Richard Kelly, US, 2001)
Bend It Like Beckham (Gurinder Chadha, UK, 2002)

This case study offers students the opportunity to look at the ways in which they are represented as a specific social group by mainstream cinema. By examining a number of recent films, students' awareness of the ways in which a film's messages and values are influenced as much by *who* is creating the representation as by the groups that are being represented, can be raised. The case study can also raise awareness of how important of teenage audiences are to film producers and how film products are being tailored to their perceived needs.

One could argue that most mainstream films released in the last 30 years have been teen films because teenagers make up much of the filmmakers' target audience. However, the term 'teen film' has tended to be reserved for those films directly exploring teenage lifestyles, offering clear identification with teenage protagonists and seeming sympathetic to the tensions that exist between the teenage and the adult world. Often these tensions are explored by focusing on characters in transition between the two worlds – involved in a rite of passage – while the narrative structure of the film highlights the protagonist's struggle to come to terms with the demands and responsibilities imposed by the adult world. Most commonly, a significant or extraordinary event will allow the protagonist to deal with these responsibilities, embrace their newfound maturity and become a 'good' citizen.

Another frequent narrative strand places a teenage protagonist in an alien environment, such as a new town or high school, where we see them struggle to adapt to this community. Again, this type of narrative tends to resolve itself with integration, as the protagonist learns the positive benefits of conformity and social responsibility or, occasionally, the community learns to become a more liberal and inclusive environment (for example *Footloose* (Herbert Ross, US, 1984) and *Pleasantville* (Gary Ross, US, 1998)).

It is obvious from this briefest of summaries that teen films tend to rely on fairly conservative value systems, emphasising the transitional nature of teenage values and implying their subordination to more responsible 'adult' values. Although the diegeses of teen films are frequently marked by either an absence of adult characters or a preponderance of inept adult characters, there is generally an authoritative older voice to guide the protagonist into making the right choices. Audiences are encouraged to identify with this learning process and to celebrate the role of society in 'teaching' the teenager to belong.

Background

Teen films reflect the emergence of the teenager as a distinct social and economic force. In the aftermath of World War II, a prolonged period of political stability and prosperity and wider social access to college education created a generation of young men and women with money, time and a need to define themselves as a specific group who were no longer children, but for whom the world of work and family were not yet suitable options. Tensions caused by this upheaval were quick to emerge in the popular cultural products of the time, particularly in film. *Rebel Without A Cause* (Nicholas Ray, US, 1955) focused on teen characters set adrift in a world where conventional notions of masculinity and authority were loosing their relevance. Films such as *The Wild One* (Laszlo Benedek, US, 1953) and *The Blackboard Jungle* (Richard Brooks, US, 1955) indicate that concerns about the negative impact of teenage behaviour, with its lack of respect for adult authority are not merely 21st-century phenomena, but were equally marked in 1950s' society.

The range of teenage representations expanded as cinema audiences changed and production companies chased the teenage dollar more consistently. More and more films began to focus exclusively on teenage lifestyles and the high school became a common location, serving as a microcosm of the teenage community. Similarly, the inhabitants of this community began to splinter into easily recognisable groups and stereotypes – jocks, geeks, rich kids, stoners, and so on – that persist into many contemporary films. In most teen films, the protagonist is forced to negotiate with these groups, sometimes sympathetically and sometimes aggressively, generally as part of a process of asserting their individuality. This allows the teen film to target its audience with a clear sense of the importance of personal identity (a message that is particularly pertinent to the teenage viewer), while still promoting the need to integrate into a wider community: to put it tritely, 'be yourself, but don't be too different'.

Given the clarity of the genre's core values and the profit potential of allowing teenagers the pleasure of watching themselves on screen, it is unsurprising that the teen film has been adapted to a wide range of generic templates, creating hybrids that look to further develop the audience base. The rites-of-passage drama has been a staple approach since the 1950s, but has been inflected through different gender, class and ethnic backgrounds. The same kind of narrative structure has frequently been explored through different kinds of comedy, ranging from the gentle *Stand By Me* (Rob Reiner, US, 1986) to the gross out *American Pie* (US, 1999–2003) trilogy. The teen film has also shown itself to be flexible enough to accommodate hybridization with horror (such as *A Nightmare on Elm Street* (Wes Craven, US, 1984), *The Faculty* (Michel Mann, US, 1999)), science fiction (such as *Back to the Future* (Robert Zemeckis, US, 1985), *Donnie Darko*), fantasy (such as *Labyrinth* (Jim Henson, US, 1986)) and even art films (such as *Kids* (Larry Clark, US, 1995), *Elephant* (Gus van Sant, US, 2003)).

Mean Girls

In many ways, *Mean Girls* (Mark S Waters, US, 2004) fits the template of the teen or high-school comedy very neatly. The film begins with the arrival of new student, Cady, who has to adapt to a high-school life dominated by cliques. In the process, she falls in love and learns important lessons about herself and her relationships with others, marking her movement towards maturity. Yet the film is able to carve out a distinct identity within

Mean Girls

its genre by its focus on a diegesis dominated by women and by its parodic treatment of well-established conventions and narrative episodes.

Cady arrives at high school having been home-schooled by her zoologist parents in Africa for 15 years. The film clearly indicates that she is an alien in this culture and needs to be taught the way that it works; however, little reference is made to her struggles to fit into an American way of life per se. For Cady, learning to adapt to high school is learning to adapt to American culture. The film also uses her background to draw some amusing Darwinian parallels to her situation, with the high school as an ecosystem in which adaptation and strength are the keys to survival. In a number of sequences, students literally act like animals in front of the camera to highlight the primal nature of the rituals we are observing, such as the visit to the mall, where students preen like monkeys and undertake elaborate mating rituals.

The school is controlled by the Plastics, a troika of rich, spoilt girls whose nickname implies the manipulation and artificiality of their lifestyles, compared to the 'natural' behaviour of Cady. After being allowed to eat lunch with the Plastics, who initiate her into the rules of their clique – 'You can't wear a tank top two days in a row, and you can only wear your hair in a ponytail once a week…. Oh, and we only wear jeans or track pants on Fridays' – she is prompted to infiltrate the group by Janice and Damian. Initially, the plan is to have fun at their expense; however, when Regina, the leader of the Plastics, steals the boy that Cady has fallen for, an all-out assault on the clique is planned. Despite her intentions, Cady becomes more deeply involved with the Plastics and seems to be seduced by their lifestyle.

One of the film's most obvious themes is the nature of the relationships between female characters. *Mean Girls* presents an environment that is dominated by women (this is rare in teenage films). The narrative is driven by the actions of female characters, and male characters tend to exist only as passive observers or in subsidiary comedic roles. The most substantial male role is that of Cady's gay friend Damian. Aaron, the object of Cady's affection, is little more than a trophy for the girls to struggle over, while father figures are either absent (the Plastics' fathers are obliquely referred to, but never seen), ineffective (Cady's father doesn't realise that grounding her means that she cannot go out) or unwilling to become involved in this matriarchal environment (the school principal abdicates responsibility to maths teacher Ms Norbury when faced with a female student who wishes to discuss her menstrual issues).

In contrast, female characters are clearly privileged as the main sources of the film's ideological perspectives. Hence Cady finds herself in the middle of a battle between an elitist agenda of consumer-driven individualism (represented by the Plastics) and a liberal agenda of social diversity (represented by Janice and Damian). Typically for the genre, the majority of the adult characters are marginalised as either inadequate or hypocritical and Cady is ultimately guided by the maternal figure of Ms Norbury. The teacher's status in the film is underlined by the respect she generates from both the students and other teachers. She is popular with students, running the school Mathlete programme, is both a good teacher and an attractive single woman – an awkward courtship with the school principal is hinted at.

The climax of the film concerns the discovery of the Burn Book, the Plastics' file of rumours and gossip on every member of the school community. The file is a concrete symbol of the power of hearsay as a controlling currency in the school. Regina photocopies the file and distributes its pages around the school. A tracking shot pulls back to reveal her watching in satisfaction as the school degenerates into a brawling mass of bodies as a result.

Ms Norbury's willingness to forgive Cady for the false rumour about her in the Burn Book demonstrates that empathy and acceptance lie at the heart of the film's liberal values. When Cady wins the title of Spring Princess at the annual prom, she breaks her tiara into pieces to distribute among the crowd, all of whom she believes deserve recognition for their individual worth. The clichéd and contrived nature of this scene seems to pull it towards parody of the genre's reliance on a redemptive closure. However, it is also possible to read these final scenes as confirmation of the power of community and conformism to tame the worst excesses of individualism.

Donnie Darko

Donnie Darko

Donnie Darko (Richard Kelly, US, 2001) is one of the more unusual variations on the teen-film blueprint. Part rite of passage, part science fiction and part religious allegory, it seems to offer a metaphysical exploration of the transition from teenager to adulthood that is both movingly personal and intriguingly universal. Initially, the diegesis appears to be taking us into predictable teen territory. Donnie is a troubled teenager despite being brought up in a seemingly close-knit family, in a picture-book, middle-class American town and attending a 'good' school, where he achieves intimidatingly high test scores and is nurtured by caring teachers.

Unlike his cinematic predecessors, such as Jim Stark in *Rebel without a Cause*, Donnie's angst is literalised in the form of a mental disorder akin to schizophrenia. He attends therapy, is prescribed medication, but still has visions of a disturbing rabbit-like creature called Frank, who leads Donnie into a series of destructive episodes around his community. Donnie's vandalism is not arbitrary, however. He uses elemental forces, particularly fire and water, as a way of attacking what he perceives as hypocrisy, first through the flooding of the school and then through the burning of self-help guru Jim Cunningham's house.

Early in the film, Frank lures Donnie onto a local golf course in the middle of the night, thereby saving his life as the jet engine of a passing aircraft smashes down on his bedroom while he is out. The event precipitates a spiritual and moral crisis in Donnie, as he is forced to contemplate the nature of destiny and the question of controlling forces in the universe to understand his own survival. This crisis is exacerbated by the words of Grandma Death, a reclusive old lady whom Donnie's dad almost runs down – 'We all die alone.' Donnie is drawn into researching the question of time travel, when it transpires that Grandma Death is a former schoolteacher, Roberta Sparrow, who wrote a seminal text on the nature of time and our movement through it.

Donnie's quest is for hope and certainty in a world which seems only to offer despair and double standards. The adult world he perceives at best offers ambiguous answers and at worst impossibly trite and exploitative solutions, such as Cunningham's Love–Fear exercises. When Donnie and his new girlfriend Gretchen develop a hypothetical idea for glasses which could transmit positive and beautiful images to infants as they sleep, his science teacher, Mr Monnitoff, criticises their naivety:

> Did you stop to think that maybe infants need darkness, that maybe darkness is part of their natural development?

The notion of darkness as an essential element of the human condition would resonate with many teenage audiences struggling with the realities of the transition to adulthood. As his surname suggests, Donnie is a representative of all those who share the pessimism of that transition. However, the film also allows Donnie a degree of power and redemption, balancing its cynicism with a fantasy that would be equally appealing. Thus Donnie's elemental powers, his implied super strength (he appears to bury an axe deep into a solid bronze statue) and his intelligence mark him out as a kind of superhero. When Gretchen remarks that his name is funny, like a superhero's, Donnie replies 'How do you know I'm not one?' He is also given the ability to see and understand the world more clearly than those around him. This is most obviously illustrated by the spectral trails which he sees emanating from the chests of the people he is with; they appear to be pathways which everyone follows, a visual rendering of destiny. Donnie's power and perception give him status in this world, even though it is not realised or acknowledged by the adult community, a staple of teenage fantasy fiction.

Finally, Donnie is allowed to complete his rites of passage as he comes to understand his role in the community. After the death of his girlfriend, mother and sister, he realises that he set this chain of events into motion by escaping death at the start of the film. He seems to have mastered control of time as events run backwards to the moment before the arrival of the jet engine and, as he awaits his demise, he laughs with the realisation that he has found meaning and salvation in his life.

The ambiguity of the film's closure raises many questions. It is pertinent to ask why Donnie was saved in the first place, given that all the subsequent negative events could have been avoided if he had died at the destined moment. The intervening period, however, gives Donnie the chance to live out a fantasy of teenage life: he meets a beautiful girl and makes love to her, bests the local bullies, rebels against his school and unmasks the hypocrisy of his teachers. At the end of this, he accepts that responsibility must put an end to this lifestyle and awaits the transition – the ultimate coming of age.

Bend It Like Beckham

Bend It Like Beckham differs from the other examples because it is not a high-school comedy. As one would expect in the teen-film genre, the protagonists, Jess and Jules, are shown engaged in a struggle for acceptance and autonomy, but the battleground of this conflict is the football pitch and the forces set against them are those of family. Both protagonists excel in a sport strongly associated with a particular brand of masculinity and, despite the prejudices of their families (and particularly their mothers), by the end of the film they are able to achieve status and reward in their chosen field.

Bend It Like Beckham

Jess comes from a Sikh family who cannot understand her fascination with 'that bald man', footballer David Beckham. Football serves as a complex metaphor in the film. Initially, it seems to be a symbol of assimilation, a 'Western' sport played by the younger males of the Asian communities and watched, leeringly, by the young women. As the film progresses, however, it becomes evident that the sport is not being placed in opposition to the Sikh way of life, but is rather offered as being analogous in its rituals and its energy, and its dependency upon community involvement. Although the narrative seems to be moving towards a key moment in which Jess is forced to choose between her family's way of life and her love of football, it ultimately concludes that the two should co-exist as manifestations of Jess's individuality. The juxtaposition of football and family occurs at several points. Jess's bedroom wall is dominated by a large picture of Beckham, to whom she reveals her hopes and secrets. Downstairs, her mother prays to a similarly imposing portrait of the family god, Guru Nanak. The ritualistic elements of the match, particularly the training exercises, are frequently compared to the preparations of the family for their daughter's wedding, while an extended cross-cut sequence explicitly indicates the similarities between the group dances at the wedding and the goal celebrations as Jess's team win the local championship.

The freshness of this metaphor is indicative of a film which is looking to challenge clichéd representations and narratives of Sikh lifestyles. Jess's sister, Pinkie, has been allowed to choose her own partner in a 'love match', rather than have an arranged relationship and, in one scene, Jess offers a different perspective on the concept of arranged marriages, wondering if they're preferable to a culture which encourages sleeping around. Jess's father (played by Bollywood veteran Anupam Kher) is not an authoritarian patriarch, but a concerned parent, struggling to protect his family from the tensions and difficulties of finding a role within their adopted society. His experiences of racism as a young immigrant – although a skilled cricketer, he was barred from the English club for whom he tried to play – initially led him to prevent Jess playing football, fearing that she would experience a similar defeat. However, having watched her play, he relents, giving her the chance to make something of her talent.

Jess's family's reactions are put into further context by comparison with Jules's mother, who is reluctant to allow her daughter to play football, because she fears that the team culture could encourage lesbian feelings in her daughter. Jules's mum is shown to also act out of a misplaced desire to protect her daughter. She tells her husband: 'It was terrible what they did to that Michael, going on about him and his private business in the papers like that! Oh no!' Jules's father, like Jess's, is shown to understand his daughter more fully.

Ultimately, both girls' aim is to gain scholarships to an American training programme for female footballers. This ambition is expressed early in the film when Jules shows Jess footage of the American women's team winning Olympic gold in 2000. For the two girls, America represents liberalism, equality and opportunity. It is no coincidence that the coming-of-age climax is played as another form of immigration, as the girls prepare to fly out of Heathrow, leaving their families behind in order to seize opportunity and success on a new continent. Thus the film places Jess's struggle firmly in the context of wider issues, suggesting that the film is aimed at audiences who are more diverse than the teenage target market.

Teaching suggestions

Tips

■ Students' familiarity with teen films can make analytical tasks challenging. You could overcome this by looking at films about teenagers from non-US/UK cultures and examining key similarities and differences. The Belfast-based Cinemagic Film Festival (<www.cinemagic.org.uk/index.htm>) is now not only a global hub for new teen films outside mainstream Hollywood but also a learning resource with a remit to encourage young filmmakers.

■ From an historical perspective, encourage students to understand that the 'teenager' is only a recent concept (it dates from the 1950s). Look at examples of films prior to the 1950s and see if they can locate a recognisable teen perspective. The BBC provides such clips on its Nation on Film website and students may be shocked to see their 1950s' equivalents.

■ **Worksheet 26 Pause and rewind** has details of sequences from the films which have been successfully used in class

Activities and discussions for students:

■ Compare the characters, for example, Donnie and Jess. In what ways are they struggling against the restrictions and expectations of their communities?

■ What kinds of positive and negative qualities are attributed to teenagers? See **Worksheet 27**.

■ Examine the ways in which costume functions to indicate how characters make themselves individuals.

■ There is a sense of resolution in all of the films. Consider some alternative endings and how these could change the message of each film. **Worksheet 28** should assist with this task. This sheet can be used for other genres.

■ Look at other genres that are meant to appeal to a teen audience, eg horror, sci-fi. How do these film genres reflect important values?

■ Debate: What are the most important issues facing teenagers today? What do teenagers need to be fulfilled?

■ As Donnie Darko, write a letter to a newspaper agony aunt. Then write an agony-aunt response to his problems.

- Watch *The Urban Savannah* (Matthew Cooke, Vincent Lund, UK, 2004) (on the *Real Shorts* compilation, published by the BFI) and discuss how it represents teenagers. Compare it to the scenes that highlight the animal-like rituals, such as the visit to the mall, in *Mean Girls*.
- Imagine being explorers who have just discovered your school. In a group, talk about and act out the different 'species' of teen there.
- Use digital software to represent yourself visually as a variety of different teen stereotypes.
- Imagine you are a filmmaker who wants to change the world. Create a manifesto for teenagers then discuss how this might be represented in a film. See **Worksheet 29**.

Key books

John Lewis *The Road to Romance: Teen Films and Youth Culture*, Livrenoir, 2001
Timothy Shary *Teen Movies: American Youth on Screen*, Wallflower, 2005
Stephen Tropiano *Rebels and Chicks: A History of the Hollywood Teen Movie*, Watson-Guptil, 2006

Websites

<www.filmeducation.org/secondary/Representation/index.html> a valuable site for representations of youth, very helpful from a PHSE perspective as well as in terms of media creation.
an excellent portal that illustrates the heritage of teenage movies back to the 1950s.
<hsc.csu.edu.au/pta/scansw/teen.html> a more theoretical site linking teenage movies to the development of teenage youth culture.

4 | Comic book superheroes

An examination of the issues involved in the transition from page to screen.

Links to GCSE

In both Media and English specifications, the comic book and its screen translations have consistently been seen as not worthy of study. This bias mistakenly associates 'comic' with connotations of childishness and views the genre is male-centric and limited in thematic scope. However, award-winning directors (eg Ang Lee with *The Hulk* (US, 2003)) have explored the genre and produced texts that both examine grand motifs and produce intimate drama. Students value the genre as meaningful and relevant, so refusal to consider the genre is a missed opportunity. In particular it is worth considering the 'graphic novel' – essentially a comic that strives in its artwork, language, narrative and characterisation to produce a story that is satisfying to fans and to literary and cinematic critics. Recent graphic novels and related films such as *V for Vendetta* (James McTeigue, US/Germany, 2006) have shown that such texts can carry some demanding subject matter – for example, the notion of identity, freedom and political activism. To explore the creation and development of the graphic novel you can access many portals via fans sites and the mainstream comic producers.

Focus films

Spider-Man (Sam Raimi, US, 2002)
X-Men (Bryan Singer, US, 2000)
Batman (Tim Burton, US, 1989) and *Batman Begins* (Christopher Nolan, US, 2005)

Comic books (or graphic novels) are now well-established sources for cinematic material. However, the transformation from disposable pulp fiction, via pop-culture iconography into a successful film genre has not been without difficulty. The main obstacle has been the predominant view that comics represent low culture, unworthy of serious consideration. With the rise of Cultural Studies, however, comic books, and their artwork, messages, narratives and characters become a focus of theoretical study.

In the last century, the typical 'journey' of comic book texts started with the creation of a serialised comic strip, followed by radio shows, short films, television cartoons, television dramas and finally feature films. Recently this lineage has been bypassed with the creation of fully realised superheroes that exist solely in films (as in *Unbreakable* (M Night Shyamalan, US, 2000)).

Whatever the textual form, the comic book genre is associated with loyal audiences, with loyalty developing in the teenage years and continuing into adulthood. This makes it a potentially lucrative genre, especially as teenage audiences' spending power increases. A further appeal of the comic book film is the conversion of static, sometimes non-verbal, images into fluid action with dialogue, which enables it to attract audiences beyond its loyal fan base. A legacy of characters from early comics have made the transition to films, such as Tarzan, Dick Tracy and Flash Gordon. While there are also many comic characters who do not conform to this mould – comedic characters with witty, humorous narratives, such as Dennis the Menace – the focus of this case study is the superhero genre.

Background

Perhaps the most important institutional event in the development of Hollywood comic book films leading to the creation of the 'superhero' was the legendary rivalry between the two powerhouses of the genre – Marvel Comics and DC Comics. Their competition has fuelled the creativity of the industry. Even when they have collaborated, their brands are still distinct.

DC Comics is responsible for Superman, Batman and the leading female superhero, Wonder Woman. In the post-war period, the company took advantage of the popularity of television spin-offs, which reached a nadir or high point (depending on taste) in the camp, circus-style series of *Batman* with Adam West in the title role in the 1960s. During the 1970s and 1980s, comics from the DC stable reflected political and ecological concerns as well as the growing sexual revolution and emancipation of women. The main successes of this period were the filmic versions of *Swamp Thing* (Wes Craven, US, 1982), *Wonder Woman* (Vincent McEveety, US, 1974) and *Superman: The Movie* (Richard Donner, US, 1978). The 1990s witnessed the crossover potential of comic characters. It also saw the emergence of less conventional characters from comic book series such as Sandman (traditionally an adversary to Spider-Man) and Hellblazer on screen. The reinvigoration of the *Batman* and *Superman* franchise also shows that each successive generation can find something new and interesting in these characters.

Marvel considered itself to be the upstart rival to the 'old man' of comics, DC. The rise of the Marvel empire is attributable to Stan Lee, a polymath of the comic world who created some of the most enduring comic characters, stories and identities. For many years, Marvel struggled to create a reasonable rival to Superman. Captain America, created to fight the threat of Nazism, posed the first challenge to Superman's supremacy, but the breakthrough character was Spider-Man, quickly followed by the Hulk, Daredevil, Silver Surfer and the X-Men.

The most interesting developments within the comic book genre often spring from the tension between these companies. DC develops, changes and alters its characters in keeping with social, cultural and technological changes. Marvel tends to create new characters to challenge stereotypes and preconceptions. What both companies have in common is that their story lines often cover greater thematic concerns and issues. As a result, the genre is not simply for children. The recent rise of graphic novels (eg *Hellboy* and *Constantine*) for a more adult audience is testament to this and reflects the way the mythology and 'heroes' of the comic world may be seen as modern equivalents of the ancient gods. This is why they are worthy of study – because they reflect contemporary concerns, writ large in the actions and decisions of the 'superheroes'.

Conventions

The comic book superhero genre is undoubtedly male-dominated. The stereotypical male hero is counterposed with an equally stereotypical male villain. Female characters tend to be trophies of the hero or the villain. The hero inhabits a strange in-between world where he has special powers but also desires to be normal. He may have gained his special powers by supernatural, alien or magical means, or as a result of an accident or mutation. He is abundantly gifted but often flawed; damaged by his early trauma, he is selfless in his desire to protect humanity. His heroic dysfunction reflects his inability to 'fit into' normal society.

The 'inner' struggles of the hero are reflected in 'external' struggles. With his dual identity and commitment to saving the world on a daily basis, he can find it difficult to cope with the trivial demands of job, family and friendships. Paradoxically, he often has his most interesting conversations with his male antagonist. Although opposites, they have much in common. The villain has forgone the comforts of job, family and friendships because he is committed to ruling or destroying the world.

Spider-Man

The trials and tribulations of youth are core material for the superhero genre. The most famous and successful of these 'teen' heroes is Spider-Man. The difficult transition from muddled adolescent to maturity is reflected in the Alter Ego, Peter Parker. The archetypal, unpopular science nerd, he lacks a male role model, hesitates to express his love for Mary Jane, with his anxieties reflecting a contemporary experience of adolescence. The last thing he needs is to be bitten by a radioactive spider.

All these themes come to the fore in the cinematic rendition of the *Spider-Man* story. Peter, played by Toby Maguire, lives a somewhat impoverished life with big ambitions. He wants independence from the folksy security of Uncle Ben and Aunt Martha, to marry the beautiful, talented and popular Mary

Spider-Man

Jane, go to college and have a successful career. Peter, though, is often isolated, fretful and preoccupied. He is a sideline witness to many of the things that he desires. This makes the guise of the spider appropriate. The creature is both admired and reviled, acknowledged and feared. The Spider-Man persona represents the inner and external struggles of the outsider for acceptance. This mirrors puberty's issues of change and development.

When Peter does begin to discover his powers, it is the equivalent of a boy waking up one day and finding out that his voice has broken. Peter tests his new physique and skills to varying degrees of success or embarrassment, jumping, climbing and web-slinging, trying to come to terms with his new powers and responsibilities. This is reflected in one of the central moments of the film: when Peter lies to his surrogate father, Uncle Ben, about his motives and changing personality, Ben comments that with 'great power, comes great responsibility'. These words come back to haunt Peter when his churlish inaction against a robber leads to Ben being murdered. This is a seminal moment in the *Spider-Man* narrative as it speeds Peter's development into a crime fighter, albeit a reluctant one.

This conflict between selfishness and nobility, between egotism and sacrifice is the main motif of the film. Many of the other characters experience this impasse. It is also the point (like in many other films) where the hero and the villain meet. When the Green Goblin offers Peter a deal to join forces and rule the world, Spider-Man remembers the words of Uncle Ben and rejects the offer. However, if Peter has any natural ally in the film, it is the Green Goblin. The villain is a businessman driven by the need to be successful. His ambition caused the accident that led to Norman Osborne's transformation into the Green Goblin. This has an inverse effect. Osborne becomes unstable, unpredictable, ill-tempered and juvenile. As Peter is an adolescent struggling to become a man, Osborne is a man struggling not to act like an adolescent.

While all of these messages and meanings are subtly portrayed, the backbone of this comic film is the challenges and dramas of adolescence, appealing to the target audience: the adolescent male and the mature male recalling the tribulations of adolescence.

X-Men

A generally inaccurate criticism of the comic-book superhero genre is that it does little to represent the views of minorities, the disenfranchised or those who exist outside the mainstream. Many comics (especially DC's) have tackled issues such as homelessness, AIDS and disability.

X-Men

The representation of women is more contradictory. While most comics give the impression that females are adjuncts without an existence in their own right, there are examples of significant female heroes, for example, Electra and Catwoman. In their narratives, they struggle for independence, against villains who attempt to control them. However, as secondary characters in the wider narratives of *Daredevil* and *Batman*, they lack a stand-alone value among fans and aficionados. Even the *X-Men* (US, 2000–6) franchise, where women are at the centre of the narrative, undermines them by the positioning of men in roles of power and influence.

The X-Men form a covert group of 'accidental' superheroes, named after their leader, Charles Xavier. Their powers derive from mutations that set them outside 'normal' society, becoming a powerful metaphor for all forms of social exclusion and prejudice. Yet, many of the female roles remain secondary, often despite the strength of their characters in the comic book-series – as in the case of Jean Grey/Phoenix, who saves Xavier's life. There is also Storm, who can control the elements and the weather, but in the film often acts as nothing more than a glorified wind machine; and Rogue, who possesses perhaps the most significant power – the ability to emulate any mutant power, yet in the film dwindles to a valuable asset to be fought over, rather than a self-realised character. On the villainous side, the most significant female character is Mystique, with the ability to masquerade as any mutant, but who of follows the lead of a man (Magneto) due to their Svengali relationship.

On the surface, there is a sense of fraternity and sorority. When the superheroes are in battle they co-operate and co-plan their actions. In the final sequence, each character combines their powers to set themselves free. It is typical though that the male character, Wolverine, is the one who stars in the final showdown and is responsible for saving humanity. It is telling that, when he is recovering, it is Jean Grey who is tending and nursing him.

Thus the women tend to be the props, complainers, love interests, victims, prizes or drain on resources. For *X-Men 3: The Last Stand* (Brett Ratner, US/UK, 2006), Halle Berry refused to participate until her character Storm was given a more significant role, her main complaint being that Storm existed solely as an accessory. The fact that Berry had to appeal for better representation is a clear indicator of how women are generally portrayed.

This then leaves the question – are comic-book films predisposed and biased against women? If they are, the reason is attributable to the fact that these texts are mostly produced by males for males, so that, irrespective of the powers of the female characters, they are still rendered powerless. This tendency is not unique to the comic-book genre but is arguably rife in the film industry as a whole.

Batman and *Batman Begins*

Batman can be seen as the James Bond of the comic-book genre. He is the ultimate gentleman detective, relying on physical prowess, psychological guile and a motivation fuelled by a dark desire for revenge. As with Bond, various actors have played the character for successive generations, each keeping the character recognisable to existing fans while appealing to a new generation.

Batman

Batman and his alter ego, Bruce Wayne, have a permanency that inspired many different celluloid versions over the years. The first film version of *Batman* (Lambert Hillier), was made by Columbia Pictures in 1943, only four years after the creation of the original comic-book version. The early *Batman* films were faithful reproductions of the comic-book narrative, appealing to a juvenile audience in search of escapism during the war. The dogged determination of Batman and his sidekick, Robin, to fight crime and the evils of society (while playing down the vigilante side of the character) continued until the early 1960s. With the 60s' counterculture and the growing economic power of teenagers, Batman was adapted. The first television version, starring Adam West as Batman, played to American and then to global audiences. Made by 20th Century-Fox from 1966–8, it was a product of its time, featuring garish colours, comedic knowingness, pantomime villainy and a camp style that made the series laughable for the wrong reasons. This move away from the source material to satisfy changing public tastes shows how fragile a franchise can be and how it can easily lose its appeal. The franchise fell dormant until the 1980s.

Perhaps reflecting the corporate greed and industrial rapacity of the 1980s, Tim Burton's *Batman* (US, 1989) was harder, darker, and more threatening and serious in its intent. Having Burton, an animator/director, who was familiar with the legacy of the character and its hidden depths, meant that the style of this version was also more comic-like. Loyal fans were in uproar over the casting of the diminutive comedian, Michael Keaton. However, his portrayal of a tortured loner (now without his sidekick) was a big success with the audience and thus at the box office. The inevitable sequel, *Batman Returns* (Tim Burton, US, 1992) was a (financial) disappointment in comparison.

There followed a nadir for the franchise. Creative differences led to the loss of Burton and the appointment of Joel Schumacher. The following films – *Batman Forever* (US, 1995) starring Val Kilmer, and *Batman & Robin* (US, 1997) starring George Clooney, with the high-profile villains, Jim Carrey as the Riddler and Arnold Schwarzenegger as Dr Freeze – were financially successful, but the franchise had lost its appeal, disappointing both the mainstream and niche audience. The re-emergence of secondary characters such as Robin and Batgirl also detracted from the isolation of the central character.

While the franchise was considered to be damaged by this period, after some time to rework the narrative for a new generation and for the old generation to forget (or forgive) past directions or interpretations, the latest *Batman* feature, *Batman Begins* (Christopher Nolan, UK/US, 2005), has met with critical and box-office success. The film shows a desire to return to the source material (as suggested in its original title – *Batman: Year One*). The narrative follows the development of the Batman persona, his training and tutelage. The ever-changing Batman logo indicates a return to a hard edge and suggests danger and controlled anger. The casting of Christian Bale, previously known for muscular and intense characters, indicates a respect for the original story.

Teaching suggestions

Tips

- Begin by looking at source 'comic' material. Many towns and cities now have a specialist comic shop. Students may also wish to show their own comic books.
- Try to look at both male and female heroes – to counter the notion that comics are only a male enthusiasm.
- Comics are not just visual experiences but rely heavily on dialogue, back story and a continuing diegesis. Comic characters have a past and present.
- Discuss the unwritten future of the stories. Think about the tension that exists between the need for continuity and the need to appeal to new generations.
- Give students the opportunity to create their own comic world. They may develop some highly personal, sophisticated and inventive ideas. This could be made cross-curricula through co-operation between Art, Media and English classes.
- **Worksheet 30 Pause and rewind** supplies details of sequences from the films.

Activities and discussions for students

■ Compare the characters: examine the characters of Xavier and Magneto (or other hero/villain oppositions). Why is one supportive and one antagonistic towards humanity?

■ Comic strips are often colourful and vibrantly two-dimensional. How do the films translate this?

■ Comic-book heroes are often crime fighters and dispensers of justice. What do these films suggest is 'good' or 'right' behaviour and what do they consider to be 'wrong' behaviour, deserving of punishment? Do some comic heroes deserve to be brought to justice themselves?

■ Look at animated versions of comic-book heroes, such as *Batman*, *Spider-Man* and *X-Men*. How do they differ from their live-action versions? What can they do that live versions can't?

■ Comic strips: sketch a comic-book character and their back story. Sketch a story – there is no need to be a good artist – with speech bubbles for dialogue. Plan a shoot for a live-action version. See **Worksheets 31–3**.

■ Hero and alter ego: Most comic-book heroes have a dual identity. Create a new hero character and the ordinary character that he/she hides behind. See **Worksheet 34**.

■ Some superheroes have almost godlike strengths and abilities. How do they use their powers?

■ Bruce Wayne takes on the identity of that which he most fears – a bat. Write about the five most scary things.

■ Imagine being a concerned parent, worried that a son or daughter is a secret superhero. In pairs, role play a conversation between concerned and inquisitive parents. Add a third person to play the son/daughter trying to hide the truth.

Key books

Milo Bongco *Reading Comics: Language, Culture and the Concept of the Superhero*, Garland Science, 2000
David Hughes *Comic Book Movies*, Virgin Books, 2003
Gina Miriroglu *The Superhero Book: The Ultimate Encyclopaedia of Comic Book Icons and Hollywood Heroes*, Visible Ink, 2004

Websites

a hub featuring information about 'seminal' superheroes and their film translations.
<www.comicstofilm.com> a range of links to all comic-to-film sites.
<www.comicbookmovie.com> another range of links to all comic-to-film sites.

5 | Sound and fury: Adapting Shakespeare

Analyses of the issues involved in adapting Shakespeare for a mass market.

Links to GCSE

- All GCSE English specifications have a mandatory component on Shakespeare. A useful resource for teaching with Shakespearean film at GCSE is the 16+ source guide by Anastasia Kerameos and Andrew Ormsby published by the BFI. It is an excellent starting point, containing a significant range of material on recent releases and classic versions. One advantage of using the films is that many exam boards no longer insist on students reading the whole play and are issuing 'extracted' texts. The film versions can elucidate the whole play, avoiding a fragmentary knowledge of the plays.

- In contrast, Media GCSE specifications generally avoid references to Shakespearean films. This division between English and Media syllabi is discussed further in the literary adaptation case study on p130.

Focus films

10 Things I Hate About You (Gil Junger, US, 1999)
She's the Man (Andy Fickman, US, 2006)

The main challenge for any cinematic rendition of Shakespeare is the process of 'translation'. Cinema has its own language and grammar and the difficulty of transforming the verbal into the visual, imagery into image, the dramatic into the kinetic presents a significant challenge to filmmakers. The practical need to abbreviate and abridge four- or five-hour plays into a more palatable viewing time also presents problems. Add to this the reverence for the

William Shakespeare's Romeo and Juliet

greatest writer in the English language and it would seem that anyone would be wary of tackling 'the Bard'.

But the motivations for doing so are manifold. In the early days of cinema, using Shakespeare as source material offered respectability to the newer medium. Filmmakers also want to pit their art against the 'measuring' stick of Shakespeare. This clash of 'high-culture' values and 'low-culture' media has been central to many Shakespeare adaptations. There is also a culture clash between the most 'English' of art forms and the most American of art forms. Another motivation could be to educate the masses. It is ironic that filmmakers can be accused of disrespect in their treatment of Shakespeare's plays when Shakespeare himself reworked and repackaged existing narratives for his audience.

Cinema tends to be financially more successful than theatre. A theatre run of a Shakespeare play may make thousands; a cinematic version may make millions. As Shakespeare plays are designed for the stage, they tend not to require high budgets (for on-location filming, etc) and can generate good revenue (especially if a big star takes standard Equity pay for their part). Finally, many adaptations are actor-driven, often 'vanity projects' that are tolerated by studios, only because the star will return (after proving their dramatic credentials) to the more economically trustworthy genres. (For example, Mel Gibson insisted on doing *Hamlet* (Franco Zeffirelli, US/France, 1990) in exchange for signing on for *Lethal Weapon 3* (Richard Donner, US, 1992).) Fortunately, Shakespeare's work is more than likely to survive all permutations and assaults on its language, symbolism and subject matter.

Background

In the silent era, the bold use of imagery and stylistic transitions showed how Shakespeare's plays could translate into the new medium of popular cinema. (See the BFI DVD *Silent Shakespeare* and <www.screenonline.org>.) To begin with, Shakespeare films were silent recordings of the stage plays, featuring renowned actors of the time. Studios who took a risk on feature-length versions quickly realised that the expressiveness of the language could be reinforced by the imaginative use of camera positions, angles, and editing. Bringing audiences familiar with theatrical versions close to performers who had previously been distant (such as Mary Pickford and Douglas Fairbanks in *The Taming of the Shrew* (Sam Taylor, US, 1929)) was fresh and innovative.

Other films, such as *Romeo and Juliet* (George Cukor, US, 1936), gave the audience faithful renditions, satisfying as performances rather than as visual experiences. This has been one of the enduring issues in Shakespeare adaptations – how best to involve the camera and enhance the 'actualities' of the original play. In productions such as *Julius Caesar* (Joseph L Mankiewicz, US, 1953), an indirect attack on McCarthyism, and the seminal *Henry V* (Laurence

Olivier, UK, 1944), a Technicolor call for patriotism in wartime, cinema versions began to 'employ' Shakespeare to suit their own artistic or political agendas rather than merely play homage to the poet.

Perhaps the greatest exponent of stretching the boundaries of Shakespeare's plays on film was Orson Welles. In his versions of *Macbeth* (US, 1948) and *The Tragedy of Othello: The Moor of Venice* (US, 1952) setting, lighting, atmosphere and camera all contributed to depicting the characters' dispositions and emotional moods. This technical mirroring of the figurative language showed that the 'inner' landscape of the play could be portrayed through *mise en scène*, positioning and costume. This led to a further breaking of boundaries and the ultimate taboo of shortening or re-interpreting the play.

Shakespeare has also lent himself to 'musical' translations. Musical versions of the plays such as *West Side Story* (Robert Wise, US, 1961) and *Kiss Me Kate* showed a healthy impertinence and informality that invigorated the work for a youth audience. The well-known adaptations of Franco Zeffirelli with his European 'weepy' version of *Romeo and Juliet* (UK/Italy, 1968); Roman Polanski with his bleak, naturalistic, psychological *The Tragedy of Macbeth* (US/UK, 1971); and Akira Kurosawa's violent *Throne of Blood* (Japan, 1957), translating *Macbeth* into the traditional Japanese *Noh* drama, all further contributed to widening the interpretations of and audiences for Shakespeare on film. These versions showed that not only could Shakespeare adaptations carry political messages to a mass market, but they could transverse international and cultural boundaries. This is one area where cinema has benefited theatre – by spreading an awareness of Shakespeare's work to a global audience.

The rise of television and home-recording technology presented a challenge to cinema and to theatre. Filmic adaptations of Shakespeare subsided after their heyday in the 1960s and 70s. Two phenomenon have helped to reinvigorated the genre. The first are the works of Kenneth Branagh, an actor and director as comfortable with the rules of the theatre as with the conventions of film. His adaptations in the late 1980s and the 1990s demonstrated the ideal equation for successful 'traditional' film versions. This involved a unified visual style, a cast of British stage stars and American film stars, a willingness to reinterpret some sections of the play purely visually, and an approach that meant that the final result satisfied as a play and a film.

The second is the electric and mimetic version of *William Shakespeare's Romeo + Juliet* by Baz Luhrmann (US/Canada, 1996). This film showed, through the use of language and iconography wrapped up in a modern intertextuality, that the work of Shakespeare was alive to constant reinterpretation. The following glut of 'teen' versions of the plays in the 1990s, such as *10 Things I Hate About You* and *O* (Tim Blake Nelson, US, 2001), showed that there is a mass youth audience with an appetite for these enduring tales. They also show that the very best

Shakespeare adaptations are the ones that unite the strengths of both the Bard and the blockbuster. Over-respectful versions are often criticised for being too theatrical, while oversimplified versions are often criticised for being too shallow and lacking the linguistic muscularity of the original.

One text that appeared to satisfy this paradigm was the extremely successful (with critics as well as audiences), *Shakespeare in Love* (John Madden, US, 1998). Although an adaptation of Shakespeare's 'supposed' personal history, it is authentic in its recreation of the time, without neglecting the need to make the film involving to the audience. Consider: if Shakespeare existed today, would he choose cinema, arguably the most successful art form of the 20th century, to express his themes and artistry?

10 Things I Hate About You

In recent years, there have been few literal remakes of the Shakespearean classics. Mainstream Hollywood prefers to use teen comedy as a vehicle for carrying the humour of Shakespeare's work and to entertain through its use of verbal sparring, cross-gender confusion and the twisted love affairs of young lovers. *10 Things I Hate About You* reflects this

10 Things I Hate About You

trend in borrowing the conventions of the teen comedy and applying them to an interpretation of *The Taming of the Shrew*.

The text merits study because it retains much of the verve and dynamism of the original, especially in the sparring and conflicted relationship between the rather playfully named, Patrick Verona (Heath Ledger) and Kat Stratford (Julia Stiles). Cross-references also abound in the name of the school (Padua High) and the use of songs and hip-hop music to create interludes that would usually precede the end of each act in the play. In many respects, this lightness of approach is necessary, because many of the ideas in the original play would be unacceptable to modern audiences. In Elizabethan England, the notion of the rebellious woman who challenged the accepted order and needed to be subdued by domesticity was comic. In modern times, the notion of an independent and self-reliant female is far from shocking. This 'cultural' anomaly is a problem for a filmmaker: How do you transpose what was once controversial and therefore highly dramatic into a time when values have changed and advanced? Perhaps this is why the the teen comedy genre proves so attractive. The humour in the situation is allowed to come to the fore, while the meta-philosophical, almost sociological aspects of

Student worksheets to support this guide are supplied at: **www.bfi.org.uk/tms**

Shakespeare recede into the background. What is more important for a modern audience is that the translation should retain the flavour and élan of the original comedy.

The case is also true for tragedies, where the most important thing to emphasise is the sense of thrill, threat and foreboding. The film, *O*, an adaptation of *Othello*, illustrates this point well in that it focuses on recreating the thematic drive of the original play and capturing the sense of rivalry between the protagonists through the sporting arenas of the teenage world. It is also a purposeful point of contrast in the casting of Julia Stiles as Desi Bramble. While Stiles' character stays one-dimensional, only expressing the baseline emotions like cynicism and anger, In *10 Things I Hate About You*, in *O*, Stiles' manages to breathe new life into the original play. This might be a result of the actors preparing and rehearsing in a stage atmosphere before shooting. Stiles' performace of tragic passion, ignorance and naivety is just as effective as any traditional 'stage' Desdemona.

The following quotes from *10 Things* demonstrate the criticism levelled at many adaptations – that they jettison the language of Shakespeare:

> Cameron: I burn, I pine, I perish (from the original play)
> Michael: Of course you do!
> Michael: Sweet love, renew thy force
> Patrick: Don't say s**t like that to me. People can hear you.

However, the charm, wit and engaging nature of the main characters arguably makes the loss of much of Shakespeare's language and meaning excusable. As the antisocial Kat, Stiles is a foil to Ledger's antisocial Patrick. Each is an outsider hiding a sensitive soul, hampered in their desires by the machinations of others and their inability to express their true selves. The battle of the sexes and their struggle for dominance is explored within the film through the dialogue and the secondary storylines of Kat's sister, Bianca and her stuttering romance with Cameron. By retaining these contrasting characters the text is true to the original and provides the audience with some interesting and involving gender questions about the sometimes caustic and complementary of behaviour of men and women.

She's the Man

She's the Man (Andy Fickman, US, 2006) followed in the footsteps of *10 Things I Hate About You*. The same scriptwriters (Leslie McCullah and Lutz Smith) wrote this version of *Twelfth Night*, following the template established in *10 Things* by transfering the courtly atmosphere of

She's The Man

royal households to the world of the teen comedy. It toys with the original play by borrowing its names (Viola played by Amanda Bynes, Olivia and Sebastian played by Laura Ramsey and James Kirk) and locations (Illyria Prep School for the kingdom of *Twelfth Night*). It also retains the central conceit of a woman masquerading as a man in a man's world (here the world of football). Lastly it references the play's alternative title (*What You Will*) and Malvolio's appearance in yellow stockings. Again, this 'pick-and-mix' of old and new dominates the character arcs, the narrative and the resolutions.

She's the Man has proved to be much more successful than the previous more faithful filmic version, *Twelfth Night* (Trevor Nunn, UK, 1999), featuring a cast of British classical theatrical talent under the aegis of a premier theatre director. Even though this is arguably the superior film version (nominated for two international film awards), it didn't reach a wide audience. Its box-office gross in the US (still a recognised barometer for international success) was $600,000. In contrast, the US box-office gross of *She's the Man* was $34 million. One reason for this success is its PG-13 MPAA rating (PG in the UK).

Sanitising the sexual content of the original into innuendo and crass humour is another strategy in making a successful Shakespearean adaptation. *She's the Man* is 'safe' in a way that Shakespeare never was in his narratives and portrayals. Even though there is still evidence of romantic triangles and stretched logic, the film version avoids much of the ribaldry that peppers the original play. The cross-dressing and barely concealed homoerotic overtones of the original text are turned into the types of jokes associated with 'gross-out' comedy. It also avoids any darkness associated with deflated expectations and unrequited love. Nevertheless, the script cleverly works in a number of references:

> Duke: It's just like the Coach says.... Be not afraid of greatness. Some are born great, some achieve greatness, some have greatness thrust upon them.

The text also mocks its own pretensions and nods knowingly at an audience who knows that we are being manipulated through generic twists and turns:

> Principal Gold: Sexual tension … male/female dynamics … all part of the High school experience!

Summary

To conclude, the main problem facing any Shakespearean adaptation is how to keep the *esprit du jour* without producing something which is not *au courant*. Each generation has been inclined to adapt Shakespeare's plays to the preoccupations and potent forms of their times. More recently, this has sometimes meant transplanting the original text to the modern teen comedy/drama, excising many of the intricacies and subtleties of the original. Even though this deprives audiences of the full experience of Shakespeare, it is more likely to attract wider audiences and guarantee financial successes.

Modern Shakespearean adaptations show, that even though Shakespeare is considered to be representative of the 'dead, European, white men' that dominate the literary classroom, he can still be a reliable source of lively narratives for a contemporary audience. Maybe this is because modern versions tap into that element of rebellion and innovation that made Shakespeare's work so popular in his own time. Even if the price we pay is a loss of poetry, figurative language and grand ideas, we are rewarded with the boisterousness and energy that comes from condensation and truncation. To put it more simply, the best adaptations may change the scenery and language but, by staying true to the circumstances, they prove their true worth.

Food for thought

Which scenario is preferable in terms of protecting the Bard's legacy? Simplified versions which are artistically dubious but which are popular and commercially alive and viable, or exact renditions which are less popular and which may even discourage further interest? With a number of versions in current production (such as *Come Like Shadows* – a version of *Macbeth* directed by John Maybury, starring Sean Bean; and *Gnomeo and Juliet* – an animated version directed by Lil' Jon with Kate Winslet voicing Juliet) the question is likely to persist.

Teaching suggestions

Tips

- Students need to understand that Shakespeare was the popular entertainment of its time. With some historical research, you could convince them that Shakespeare was about mass-market appeal and not pure elitism.
- Should students read the plays in their entirety and then watch the films? Should they be considered of equal status and worth? Some Media teachers believe that modern cinema is a vastly superior vehicle to realise the whimsy, wonder and boldness of Shakespeare's plays. They see cinema as the best form to express the true range of his creativity. Some English teachers blame cinema for becoming a distraction to live performance and undermining the position of Shakespeare with diluted and inferior versions of his texts and are particularly suspicious of the growing inclination to 'crib' Shakespeare by watching the film version rather than tackling the text. As teachers, we must make judicious choices over what we want students to watch and read – often based on time, class ability and the level of achievement desired.
- **Worksheet 35** has details of sequences from the films.

Activities and discussions for students

- Compare the characters: Romeo was a young Italian prince. How does DiCaprio's version compare to the original character?
- *A Midsummer Night's Dream* deals with the world of fairies and the supernatural. How does the film *A Midsummer Night's Dream* (Michael Hoffmann, US/Germany, 1999) represent these elements?
- Death and murder are significant elements of Shakespeare plays. How are they represented in film such as *O* and Baz Luhrmann's *William Shakespeare's Romeo + Juliet*?
- *West Side Story* is a musical version of *Romeo and Juliet* and was highly popular in its time with a youth audience. How does it compare to Baz Luhrmann's version?
- Love is often the key motivator in Shakespeare plays. What kinds of love are there in the film adaptations? Is love a strong enough justification for the actions it causes?
- Choose a secondary character from one of the films. Write a letter to the director complaining about the size of the part and explain why it deserves to be treated with more respect. Use the play to support your comments.
- Shakespeare plays often have asides to the audience. Imagine you and a classmate are a buyer and seller of a rare object. Converse and negotiate. Then whisper your asides to the audience about what the other character does not know and how you plan to rip them off.
- ICT is a great means of creative support. Students can design a film poster for a Shakespeare play they are unfamiliar with.
- See **Worksheet 36**: Write down extracts of Shakespeare dialogue and translate it into a modern idiom.
- See **Worksheet 37**: Condense a Shakespeare play into three minutes.

Key books

Richard Burt, Lynda Boose (eds) *Shakespeare the Movie II: Popularizing the Plays on Film, TV, Video and DVD*, Routledge, 2003

Deborah Cartmell *Interpreting Shakespeare on Screen*, Palgrave Macmillan, 2000

Russell Jackson (ed) *The Cambridge Companion to Shakespeare on Film* (Cambridge Companions to Literature), Cambridge University Press, 2002

Daniel Rosenthal *100 Shakespeare Films*, BFI, 2007

Kenneth S Rothwell *A History of Shakespeare on Screen: A Century of Film and Television*, Cambridge University Press, 2000

Websites

a site with thousands of links not only on the playwright and his life but also on all versions of his plays.

<www.screenonline.org.uk/education/student/shakespeare/tour1.html> an excellent, focused journey through the Bard's work and the film versions.

<www.insidefilm.com/shakespeare.html> a short and clear article about the challenges of adapting Shakespeare for the screen

6 | Love and laughter: Romcoms

Why we like to watch film stars falling in love.

Links to GCSE

This focus of study allows you to consider issues relating to genre and to explore other issues.

- In the English GCSE specifications, there is a consideration of personal, health and social issues (PHSE). Romantic comedy is a genre that centres around relationships between men and women. The website <www.filmeducation. org/filmlib.html> provides learning materials on films that can be used to explore PHSE and citizenship issues. The study of romantic comedy can encourage students to investigate their own responses and the appeal of this genre to a range of audiences.

- In the Media specifications, film certification can be a challenging issue. For example, even though *Punch Drunk Love* (Paul Thomas Anderson, US, 2002) has a 15 certificate you may still feel it is inappropriate for GCSE viewing. This constraint can often hamper teaching with film and it is worth remembering that many students regularly watch 18 certificate films. You can navigate this problem with selective viewing or parental consent forms. Furthermore, it makes an interesting debate to have with your students. The British Board of Classification <www.bbfc.co.uk> supplies background information and explanations for the kinds of decisions taken when classifying a film.

When Harry Met Sally (Rob Reiner, US, 1989)
Notting Hill (Roger Mitchell, UK, 1999)
Amélie (Jean-Pierre Jeunet , France, 2001)
Punch Drunk Love (Paul Thomas Anderson, US, 2002)

The romantic comedy makes an essential contribution to the cinema experience. In the back row and sharing a bucket of popcorn, if any genre is guaranteed to make your first date melt, it is romantic comedy. Romantic comedies are an amalgam or subgenre of two genres – the comedy and the romance. Comedies are designed to make viewers laugh and often feature ludicrous situations, witty dialogue, funny characters and the challenges and cheers of life. Comedies allow audiences to forget their own tribulations and feel uplifted. The romance film conventionally follows the story of the beginning, complication and final realisation of love between two people. Films that are sad and tragic are labelled 'melodramatic' or 'weepy'. If they focus on the emotional experience of girls or women, and their empowerment, they may be called (in a somewhat derogatory way) 'chick flicks'. These elements combine to create the potent mix of the romantic comedy.

Romantic comedies, or romcoms, are basically battles of the sexes, often with a Cinderella- or Pygymalion-type narrative. The romcom has a basic, even simplistic or formulaic, narrative: two individuals are brought together (often against their will or as an accident of fate). They may fight each other, even though there is scarcely concealed mutual attraction, while various obstacles prevent the smooth progress of their affair. The comedy revolves around their shared but often resisted or thwarted desire to be together. This leads to frustration, break-ups, and sometimes, tragic misunderstandings until they finally realise that the other is 'the one'. After a grand gesture, coincidence or declaration of love, they usually embrace or kiss; cue happy ending, often in a spectacularly 'romantic' location. Audiences like romantic comedies because they can expect a happy ending, which is a form of escape and release from the mundane.

Background

Romantic comedies are far from a modern phenomenon and were a proven format well before the advent of cinema. The structure and style of these texts share many of the features of classic literature, including Shakespeare, Jane Austen, 18th-century comedy and the parlour comedies of Wilde and Shaw. From these traditions, romantic comedy films have borrowed, in particular, the triadic structure of introduction, complication and resolution. The humorous and sardonic language is laid over the 'push/pull' or 'will they/won't they' tension of a couple in love, and the 'oppositional' nature of their personalities, physical types and even occupations. Conflicting status and ideologies often characterise the romantic comedy. This is apparent even in the early silent films. Chaplin's tramp frequently attempted to win the heart of a girl while overcoming the obstacles of poverty, rank and lack of social respectability. A lot of the films of the time were preoccupied with the intensity of the silent screen kiss and the tragedy of doomed passion. With the advent of sound and therefore a greater range of expression, romances took on a more comedic character. However, the main engine of romantic comedies has always been the pairing of stars with 'chemistry': these screen couples offer the illusion of a 'real' relationship threatened with being thwarted or undermined.

These elements are at play in what is hailed as the first truly successful Hollywood romantic comedy, *It Happened One Night* (Frank Capra, US, 1934), pairing Claudette Colbert and Clark Gable. This road comedy places an heiress and journalist on the run from their problems, only to discover that they love each other despite their differences. It is no accident that this text was so popular during a time of economic depression – the message that love will conquer all is highly effective in countering the daily fears and anxieties of the audience. This film set the tone for perhaps the next 30 years, as romantic comedy relied heavily on the pairing, situation and 'screwball' physical comedy with verbal cut and thrust. Throughout this time, the main player in this relationship was invariably male: often James Stewart or Cary Grant (in Hollywood). The bias towards casting women to complement the male star is one of the more controversial issues of the genre and not many actresses have been able to challenge this situation.

The most successful romcom duo in the 1940s Hollywood was Spencer Tracy and Katharine Hepburn. This screen team highlighted the burgeoning social emancipation of women as a result of their contributions during the war. This was in direct conflict with the accepted gender roles of the 1940s and 50s where a man was head of the household, main provider and unquestioned patriarch. It is indicative of the division between films and reality during these conservative times that audiences laughed at the pairing but would not have tolerated their off-screen affair (Tracy was a married Catholic). This shows that romantic comedy can be a safety valve, exploring themes of sexual conflict, as long as the status quo is maintained and reasserted.

In the 1960s, the most successful pairing was Rock Hudson and Doris Day (epitomised in *Pillow Talk* (Michael Gordon, US, 1959), who mainly featured in narratives of courtship or bedroom farce with a changing (but never changing) power-relationship between men and women. In the 1970s, a period of economic boom, the growing status of women, the advent of the blockbuster, and the popularity of the romantic comedy was challenged. Subsequently, films such as *When Harry Met Sally*, and pairings such as Meg Ryan and Tom Hanks, have successfully helped to revive the genre. It now often serves as a 'star vehicle' for actors such as Hugh Grant, Mel Gibson, Julia Roberts and, more recently, Jennifer Lopez.

Although successful romantic comedies are still made, the classic pairing formula has been partly displaced by the 'chick-flick' (a term that reflects male disenchantment with the genre and their preference for 'gross-out' humour). Romantic comedies are now deemed to be a female genre although historical precedent suggests that the best romantic comedies appeal to both genders.

When Harry Met Sally

When Harry Met Sally is a typical romantic comedy of mismatched lovers. The narrative revolves around the irregular meetings of Harry Burns and Sally Albright and their initial, mutual dislike, which grows into fondness and then love. This 'will they/won't they?' story is punctuated by talking-head documentary-style footage of other couples recounting how they met and fell in love. The

When Harry Met Sally

architecture of New York City provides the backdrop and the dating scene the back story. What makes *When Harry Met Sally* a modern romantic classic is its intense focus on the tribulations of relationships and the often conflicting views of men and women on love and sex, and the perpetual dilemma of how men and women resolve their competing agendas. The film's success is partly due to the effectiveness of the casting and the direction. Billy Crystal's Harry is an independent witty, cynical, pessimistic romancer. Meg Ryan's Sally is an independent, bubbly, buoyant but, at heart, troubled seeker of romance. Rob Reiner exploits these polarities to steer a trajectory from sparring couple to finally loving relationship.

Although, like most modern romantic comedies, the film readily references earlier films (especially *Casablanca* (Michael Curtiz, US, 1942)), the bedrock of the text is its witty dialogue and its use of music to match mood and trace development. These qualities are not unique to romantic comedy, but the linguistic jousting and the colouring of scenes with songs, creates a 'romantic' disposition in the audience. Music is an essential element of romantic comedy, lending a film an additional emotional dimension. Typically, Harry's declaration of love is accompanied with a swell of romantic music on the soundtrack. Music and songs often help to reflect and enhance a sense of time and place. Many songs bridge the recognition gap between old and new and work to secure a wide audience for mainstream films. In *When Harry Met Sally*, several songs are performed by music legends such as Frank Sinatra, Ella Fitzgerald and Louis Armstrong. Their blues and jazz styles are in keeping with the image of New York and the sense of soulful, blighted romance. This is a deliberate ploy by the director. According to Reiner, 'even though this was a modern love story, I wanted to give it a timeless feeling'. This is apparent in the choice of songs such as 'It Had to Be You' and 'Our Love is Here to Stay'. These types of songs often feature within the genre and act as shared emotional indicators. Having Harry Connick Jr, a would-be modern Sinatra, perform them, raises their appeal to younger audiences. The film's skilful use of sound and language punctuates and reflects the character arcs and enhances the romantic moments.

One of the most significant one-liners occurs at the beginning of the film, when Harry states that 'Men and women can't be friends because the sex part always gets in the way'. This is his rebuff to a rather irked Sally, who has already rejected his vague advances. It forms the premise of the film and gives the audience an insight into both characters' perspectives.

The dialogue is the driving force of the film. Scripted by the successful female director Nora Ephron, it creates many comic moments and helps the audience identify with the characters. The blunt, brash language, mixing sentimentality and seriousness, seems spontaneous and natural. Ephron's words are wittier, of course, but the audience, in times of romantic trouble, would love to be able to match the sharp wit of the characters. For example:

> Harry: Was it worth it? The sacrifice for a friend you don't even keep in touch with?
> Sally: Harry, you might not believe this, but I never considered not sleeping with you a sacrifice!

Broken pride and deflated ambitions often feature in romantic comedy. One character may be reaching out to the other, making themselves vulnerable with their words. This sense of bathos, impending disappointment and rejection is another reason why the audience finds the happy ending so satisfying. For example, Harry's now classic list of Sally's attributes is in keeping with the way romantic comedies voice romantic expectations and fears of rejection.

> Harry: I love that after I spend the day with you, your perfume is on my clothes … and it is not because I'm lonely, and it's not because it's New Year's Eve. I came here tonight because when you realise you want to spend the rest of your life with somebody, you want the rest of your life to start as soon as possible.

Notting Hill

The Richard Curtis and Hugh Grant partnership has proved to be one of the most commercially successful in recent romantic comedy. From *Four Weddings and a Funeral* (Mike Newell, UK, 1994) to *Love Actually* (Richard Curtis, UK, 2004), their brand of romantic comedy deals with social status, often within an Anglo-American, cross-Atlantic context.

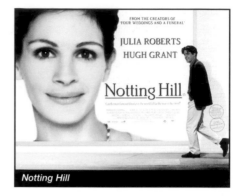

Notting Hill

In *Notting Hill* (Roger Michell, UK, 1999), Julia Roberts plays the star Anna Scott, seeking anonymity in the bookshops of Notting Hill after a bad relationship break-up. Hugh Grant plays William Thacker, the owner of a travel bookshop. Their first and second meetings are accidental coincidences typical of romantic comedy. The film offers a neat reversal of the male–female lead dynamic, with the man believing he is unworthy of the attention of the female lead. This shift is not only indicative of Roberts's star status, having come a long way from playing a prostitute in *Pretty Woman* (Garry Marshall, US, 1992), but is also a deliberate ploy on the part of the filmmakers to make Grant the butt of the jokes. Grant has made a career out of the humour that comes from English reticence and emotional discomfort. This allows the film to develop its theme of culture clash – 'cultured' versus 'uncultured', English versus American, Old World restraint versus New World emotionalism – fruitfully referencing the (apparently) contrasting perspectives of two historic adversaries and allies.

The tagline of *Notting Hill* is an accurate summary of the main quandary: 'Can the most famous film star in the world fall for the most ordinary guy?'. This plot is based on a familiar theme of romcom: what happens when a man and woman of unequal social status meet? *Notting Hill* is unusual in that it plays-up the notion of a divide by casting perhaps the most famous current female star, as (more or less) herself, and a famous male star opposite her as 'the most ordinary guy'. The effect is not only entertaining but encourages the notion that we are being given an insight into the lifestyle of the real-life Roberts, while being able to laugh at Grant's characteristics that play with his 'ordinary guy' star image. The film addresses the media 'circus' surrounding stars, opening with her character Anna being pursued by paparazzi. Two key scenes in the film show Anna Scott being interviewed by William when she mistakenly thinks he is a journalist, and at the film's climax when he sneaks into her press conference and exposes himself to the press, although he is very media-shy. These scenes derive irony from the fact that Grant and Roberts are constantly faced with the media and paparazzi as 'real' stars, but that as fictional characters Grant slips into the reporter role, while Roberts is the star trying lead an 'ordinary' life, both actually trying to avoid media exposure. There is also the added dimension of the play on the film within the film: William walks past a poster featuring Anna (Roberts!), and watches a film that stars her. Here then is a significant clash: reality versus unreality, a staple of romantic comedy reaching back to the dual personalities and 'masks' of Shakespeare's plays.

However, the comedy of difference not only extends to their professions and lifestyles but also to their perceptions of the world and relationships. After his initial meeting with Anna, William watches some of her fictional characters on video. He struggles to find the real woman behind the image. This is apparent in moments when he helps her learn lines or invites her to his sister's birthday party. In these situations, the film plays on the difficulty of the star to be perceived and treated as ordinary. Anna strives to be ordinary, commenting that she is just a 'girl looking for a guy'. She is the mythological goddess willing to step off her pedestal, the fairytale mermaid willing to step onto dry land.

The message of romantic comedy is that love can unite all these opposites and make them complementary and dynamic. If difference drives the drama, it also leads to the conclusion that difference can be overcome. Many critics have baulked at this unrealistic view. In particular, some have expressed distaste for Curtis' comedies, for their promotion of the idea that residents of upmarket areas, like Notting Hill, are somehow representative of ordinary people, that everyone has supportive family and friends and experiences little serious hardship. *Notting Hill* shows London as a place of all seasons, a village within a metropolis with a tightly knit community, where love and happiness triumph. Such a positive and idealistic message is typical for the romcom, accounts for the success of the genre and the reason why it is loved by audiences and filmmakers alike. It suggests that even in the impersonal scale of the whole world, we are connected and that, even among so many random encounters, we will find our match.

Amélie and *Punch Drunk Love*

Both *Amélie* (Jean-Pierre Jeunet, France, 2001) and *Punch Drunk Love* (Paul Thomas Anderson, US, 2002) are innovative and deliberate attempts to work against the expectations of the romantic comedy and present the audience with a more meaningful or perhaps more 'muddled' vision of love and its trials and tribulations. Each film has a romantic love at its heart, yet it is warped. The central characters, respectively, of Amélie Poulain and Barry Egan (the main character in *Punch Drunk Love*) are both damaged fantasists trapped in a mundane world, working in jobs involving selling and customer care, when neither is equipped to engage in conversation. They have both retreated from real relationships because they have been hurt in the past and their sensitivity makes them vulnerable. Both characters behave almost childlike in their encounters with others. By recoiling into infancy they attempt to control the uncontrollable – the course of true love. Many of the comedic moments of the films arise when the characters are overcome by the impact of their own meddling. Amélie brings together a work colleague and a customer, only to arouse jealousy and bitterness. Barry seeks some satisfaction in the company of others, only to end up being pursued for money and have his life threatened. This out-of-control quality is reflected in the style and music of each film, which help to create a sense of distortion, unreality and altered perspectives.

Amélie

Punch Drunk Love

Another feature of the films is the way each character attempts to battle against their own suppressed desires and the hectoring of others to conform to the ideals of 'romantic love' (as it is portrayed in romcoms). Amélie avoids contact by acting as an 'angel' to others, intervening in other people's lives while being incapable of acting on her own desires. Barry is emotionally incoherent and has violent outbursts. Each character runs away from what they most fear: intimacy, physicality and commitment. This is not the usual landscape of the romantic comedy. Here, the characters' almost psychopathic tendencies drive the story. Each yearns for an escape from a self-imposed prison and release from loneliness, but lacks the skills to dictate his/her own destiny. To gain love, they must abandon their comfort zones. Amélie uses her creativity to reveal her identity to the man she loves by leaving him a trail of clues. Barry's uses temper and propensity for violence help to protect his love from jeopardy. Even though the films escape the typical trajectory of the romantic comedy, they deliver a happy ending in the form of the lovers finding and accepting each other – for better or worse.

Teaching suggestions

Tips

- In teaching the romcom genre, you may find that female students can identify with the romantic qualities more, while male students tend to focus more on the comedic elements. These viewing responses should be challenged and questioned, using activities outlined below.
- You could also examine how cultural differences affect the representation of love, affection and relationships. US, UK and Western European romantic comedies may have similar generic traits and these could be explored. The portrayal of relationships and the battle between the sexes can help students to question their own perceptions, prejudices and views. **Worksheet 38** has details of sequences from the films.

Activities and discussions for students

- Compare the American Harry (*When Harry Met Sally*) and the English William (*Notting Hill*). How might their different views of love arise from their cultural background?
- How does Jeunet employ camerawork in *Amélie* to show connections between people and things?
- There is a musical interlude in *Punch Drunk Love* when all seems lost to Barry. Why do you think the director put it there?
- *Amélie* takes place in Paris, a city renowned for romance. How is Paris represented in this film?
- Ask the students a series of questions about what they love the most and record their answers. Use the recordings to create a definition of love.
- Discuss: Is it possible for men and women to be just friends?
- Imagine that your home city or town is the most romantic place on earth. What would be the top three most romantic places in the city and why?
- *Pretty Woman* is one of the most successful romantic comedies ever. What message do you think it sends out to young women?

Key books

Peter Evans, Celestino Deleyto (eds) *Terms of Endearment: Hollywood Romantic Comedy of the 80s and 90s*, Edinburgh University Press, 1998

James Harvey *Romantic Comedy in Hollywood: From Lubitsch to Sturges*, Knopf, 1987

Elizabeth Kendall *The Runaway Bride: Hollywood Romantic Comedy of the 1930s*, Knopf, 2002

Websites

<www.storyispromise.com/wromance.htm> a fine essay on the art of writing a romantic comedy and how this staple genre is constructed.

<www.writersstore.com/article.php?articles_id=67> another article on the generic expectations of the romantic comedy.

a portal for links and articles on the romantic-comedy genre.

7 | A picture or 1000 words: Literary adaptations

An examination of some of the techniques used to adapt prose into visual equivalents.

Links to GCSE

Prose adaptations illustrate a tension between English and Media Studies:

- The media component of most GCSE English specifications concentrates on specialist prose within media texts and on tone, address, register and language selection. In particular they tend to focus on newspapers, magazines, advertising and publicity materials. This misses an important opportunity to study rich texts that link directly with the books students might be studying.
- GCSE Media Studies specifications tend to avoid the viewing of 'adaptations' as this is seen as the realm of English teaching.
- The English and Media Centre attempts to bridge this divide (<www.englishandmedia.co.uk>) giving 'parity of esteem' to both subjects areas. The centre produces a range of free materials that consider both the literary texts and their audiovisual interpretations.

Focus films

Scrooged (Richard Donner, US, 1988) (a version of Charles Dickens's *A Christmas Carol*

To Kill a Mockingbird (Robert Mulligan, US, 1962)

Clueless (Amy Heckerling, US, 1995)

Literary adaptations are a mainstay of both film and television. For this genre, fidelity to the source material is the ever-present issue, especially if the original material is a classic, as adaptation implicitly suggests change, revision, variation and alteration. Hollywood has always relied on novels for plots and storylines but is often accused of treating the classics irreverently and, perhaps because of this, cinema tends to be seen as a poor relative of literature. It should be remembered that literature also recycles narratives and myths. Shakespeare did this, with many of his plays being re-workings of earlier stories.

Adaptations depend on the relationship between institution, audience and text. The institution hopes to gain critical and aesthetical kudos from adapting literary texts, especially classics, while audiences are curious to see how familiar stories translate onto the screen. Audiences for adaptations, however, are notoriously difficult to please. Although an adapted text may attract viewers who are loyal to the original and keen to see how it has been interpreted, the casting, omission of characters, location, scenes and subplots can leave the audience disappointed. Fans of classic novels increasingly use the internet to criticise publicly what they see as bad adaptations. But adaptations always have been popular, a fact recognised in the Academy Award for Best Adapted Screenplay.

Every year, major studios buy the rights to thousands of novels, many of which remain in 'development hell', if only to keep the competition's hands off them. By adapting a novel, studios can also bypass part of the creative process – the creation of the story and characters. Novels that are out of copyright are even easier to adapt because there is no living author (or author's estate) to insist on a particular interpretation. Interestingly, a growing number of successful books are based on films. This dynamic flux that exists between text and film is also apparent in adaptations of new types of media texts. In the last 10 years more videogames have been adapted for the screen than literature classics. This shows that cinema is always looking for fresh sources of inspiration, as well as trying to appeal to existing tastes.

Background

Filmmakers seek source material with a wide appeal and a strong narrative impetus as well as interesting characters with whom audiences can identify. Below are some of the novelists and novels whose work has been adapted into successful films.

Filmmakers are attracted to the great human stories and the epic scale and sweep of the works of the great novelists of the 19th and early 20th centuries, including Tolstoy, Hugo, Dumas, Faulkner, Twain, Hemingway and Steinbeck. Particularly popular sources for the horror film genre include Gothic novels, like *Dracula* by Bram Stoker and *Frankenstein* by Mary Shelley. *Dracula* is one of the most revisited texts in cinema. Castaway and social outsider narratives have been based on novels by such authors as Daniel Defoe (*The Adventures of Robinson Crusoe*) and Henry Fielding (*Tom Jones*).

Jane Austen's comedies of manners have proved a popular source for films partly due to their skilled observation of, and commentary on, a social milieu and women's growing desire to gain independence from the strictures of conservative family expectations. As well as more or less straightforward adaptations of her novels, there have been attempts to relocate the stories in modern times, such as *Clueless* and *Bride and Prejudice* (Gurinder Chada, UK/Germany, 2004).

Other novelists whose works have been made into successful films include William Thackeray (*Vanity Fair*) and Charles Dickens (*David Copperfield*, *Oliver Twist*, *A Christmas Carol* and *Great Expectations*). Along with Austen, Dickens's novels have been the most frequently used sources for film adaptations, including musicals and animations. Even the Muppets have remade some of his classics. The appeal of his novels lies in his ability to combine tragedy, comedy, pathos, sentimentalism and satire: all embodied in archetypal characters. The description and drama in Dickens's novels, with their reversals of fortune and surprise endings, prove a useful strategy in attracting cinema audiences.

Another wellspring of material comes from the novels of the Brontë sisters and of Thomas Hardy, with their portrayals of the fateful Victorian struggle between the pastoral past and industrial future, their expressions of repressed desire and their impassioned symbolism. *Wuthering Heights*, *Jane Eyre* and *Tess of the D'Urbervilles*, for example, have all been made into popular films.

In the 20th century, a new generation of writers explored the clash of cultures inherent in the rise and fall of the British Empire. These include the novels of Joseph Conrad, a Polish immigrant to England, with his classics, *Nostromo*, *Lord Jim* and *Heart of Darkness* (the basis for *Apocalypse Now* (Francis Coppola, US, 1979) a brilliant modern adaptation with Vietnam as the backdrop). Other authors who examined changing social mores and Britain's changing relationship with the rest of the world include D H Lawrence, E M Forster and Graham Greene. In his adaptations of *Women in Love* (UK, 1969) and *The Rainbow* (UK, 1989), Ken Russell translated Lawrence's passionate intensity for modern audiences who had experienced the breakdown in traditional moral and sexual mores. The director/producer relationship of James Ivory and Ismail Merchant produced films based on Forster's novels, such as *A Passage to India* (UK/US, 1984), *A Room with a View* (UK, 1985) and *Howard's End* (Japan/UK, 1992). The success of these films did much to stereotype the British cinema industry as purely a purveyor of costume dramas. Adaptations of Greene's novels gave audiences a sense of the seamier side of British life in the portrayal of criminality in *Brighton Rock* (John Boulting, UK, 1947), adultery in *The End of the Affair* (Neil Jordan, Germany/US, 1999), and the struggle for religious faith and personal integrity in *The Power and the Glory* (Marc Daniels, US, 1961).

In the meantime, the work of the American novelist, H G Wells, such as *The Time Machine* and *The War of the Worlds*, served to initiate the development of the science-fiction genre and, more recently, the novels of Philip K Dick were made into such sci-fi classics as *Bladerunner* (Ridley Scott, US, 1982).

Modern audiences retain an appetite for classic and current adaptations. Over the course of the 20th century, more Irish, Australian, Canadian and Caribbean literature was adapted for the screen. A new wave of contemporary writers is supplying their home industries and the Hollywood system with fresh material. To name, but a few, English writers whose novels were adapted into popular films: Irvine Welsh's *Trainspotting* (Danny Boyle, UK, 1996), Nick Hornby's *Fever Pitch* (David Evans, UK, 1996), *About a Boy* (Paul Weitz, Germany/US/France/UK 2002) and *High Fidelity* (Stephen Frears, US/UK, 2000), Helen Fielding's *Bridget Jones* (2001–4) franchise, and J R Rowlings, with her highly successful *Harry Potter* (2001–present) franchise.

Finally, it is worth mentioning *Adaptation* (Spike Jonze, US 2002), a film that teases us with the twists and turns of a scriptwriter's mind as he struggles to adapt a novel for the screen. It is a telling insight into the challenge of making literary works visually arresting.

Scrooged

A Christmas Carol has become a perennial seasonal tale with numerous film adaptations. In Dickens's original, London, suffering the oppressive effects of the Industrial Revolution, is a place of grind, poverty, loneliness and social decay. His novels served as a platform for his humanitarian opinions and desire to address social wrongs. However, as a diatribe, satire

Scrooged

or polemic on the suffering of the underclass and the ignorance of the elite is unlikely to attract an audience seeking Christmas cheer, the social critique of the original has gradually given way in the retellings to a sentimental parable of morality, mixed with a sticky layer of icing sugar.

A Christmas Carol (Edwin L Marin, US, 1938), starring Reginald Owen, is the earliest and most faithful rendition of the original. The film was made around the time that Dickens started to feature in the English canon, which may account for the 'traditional' nature of the adaptation. The Scrooge of this piece is a monstrous type, with his meanness reinforced by make-up, and a sense of coldness created by the *mise en scène*. There is a sense of threat and danger in the ghost scenes, and that of social responsibility, that is not accidental in the pre-war atmosphere of the time.

Scrooge (Brian Desmond Hurst, UK, 1951), starring Alastair Sim, is now revered as the seminal film version of the novel, balancing the bleakness of Dickens's novel with the comedic quality of Sim. His Scrooge is initially a man of unremitting negativity and selfishness who attempts to destroy the dreams of those who work for him. As the film progresses, however, his character is transformed by his growing awareness of the suffering he has caused. The film plays down the role of significant characters such as Marley and Cratchit and emphasises that of Crachit's invalid son, Tiny Tim, a picture of weak, wide-eyed innocence who has come to represent a rather laughable paragon of 'childish' virtue. The visions of alternative routes and realities are played movingly by Sim. Whether he is quivering with fear or joy, his Scrooge is human in all his faults and virtues. Subsequent versions have struggled to move away from this template.

Scrooge (Ronald Neame, UK, 1970), starring Albert Finney and Sir Alec Guinness, *A Christmas Carol* (Clive Donner, US, 1984), starring George C Scott, and *A Christmas Carol* (David Hugh Jones, US, 1999), starring Patrick Stewart, all make light of the story. London is portrayed as 'chocolate box' world in these film versions, all snow bonnets and plump turkeys on market stalls and the final over-romanticising of Scrooge's conversion is even more sickly in its message. It has become a story that provides the audience with a sense of seasonal comfort and reassurance, rather than provoking them to question their lifestyles and social responsibilities.

In contrast, *Scrooged* (Richard Donner, US, 1988), starring Bill Murray, captures the cynicism and sense of menace of the original. It also proves, with its change from Merrie England to 1980's yuppie New York, that the best adaptations are often the ones willing to reinvent the original for a modern audience. Bill Murray plays a neurotic, domineering executive who has sacrificed personal friendships and comforts for a successful career. With the often surreal setups and visitations, the film retains the message of the original and provokes reflection from the audience. By being so different from the original, the film manages to grasp the essence of the story and adapt it for a modern palate.

To Kill a Mockingbird

Harper Lee's *To Kill a Mockingbird* is a densely thematic book with the nature of good, evil, community, justice and race at its heart. The story of the main character, Scout, and her family, who live in the 'white' Alabama South during the Depression, centres on a vision of America, the home, the family and the often disturbing undercurrents that lie just beneath the surface. In many ways, the text is a precursor to films that delve behind the façade of the American Dream and its illusion of fraternity, patriotism and righteousness. The story and the development of the characters in the novel are focused on the prosecution of a black man, Tom Robinson, accused of raping a white woman, who is keen to protect her own reputation. The book is more than an examination of this scandal. Its portrayal of 1930s' America carries a message about the racial divisiveness

To Kill A Mockingbird

of the 1960s, when it was written, and the burgeoning Civil Rights movement. With their father, Atticus Finch, representing the defendant in a case that splits the community, Scout and her brother Jem are confronted with a backlash of prejudice and rejection. The novel presents a world of moral murkiness and few absolutes.

The film *To Kill a Mockingbird* (Robert Mulligan, US, 1962) is brave in delivering an unpalatable message to a mainstream audience. The relationship between Atticus (played by Gregory Peck) and the black community, shown especially in the aftermath of Atticus's famous defence speech, was considered daring in its suggestion that racial differences can be easily overcome by mutual respect and understanding. The death of Tom (Brock Peters) in captivity, and the disconcerting relationship of the children with the older and mentally challenged Boo Radley (Robert Duvall) also reflect the lack of easy resolutions. The film excises many scenes and significant characters, such as Aunt Alexandra, with the effect of distilling the story to its essentials. Some claim that the story lost something on the way. The film has also been also accused of a naïve oversimplification of race relations, with Tom as the dignified victim, Mayella as the white trash siren and Atticus as the middle-class arbiter of legitimacy and decency. Civil Rights advocates have argued that, by focusing on Atticus rather than Tom, the film implies only white people can resolve race issues. These arguments took on a wider significance with the assassination of Martin Luther King in 1968. Gregory Peck won an Academy Award for his performance, and his character, Atticus Finch, was voted the greatest screen hero of all times by the American Film Institute in May 2003 (beating Indiana Jones and James Bond).

Without doubt, the film sanitises and sentimentalises the original but, in doing so, allows its themes and values to reach a wider audience, proving that film can be a powerful vehicle for conveying the controversial ideas from an original written text.

Clueless

Jane Austen adaptations account for many popular films. In recent versions actresses such as Gwyneth Paltrow and Kate Beckinsale have starred in period costume romantic comedies that faithfully replicate the genteel Regency period. *Clueless* (Amy Heckerling, US, 1995), starring Alicia Silverstone, takes a radically different approach. Transferred from gentrified England to *nouveau riche*, West-Coast LA, the film represents a jarring contrast to *Emma*, the 1816 novel on which it is based. Yet the film is faithful to the book in bringing Austen's universal message to a very different time. And though the language and setting are different in the film, the fundamental issues stay the same.

Clueless

Emma, the novel, is primarily concerned with the witterings and intertwinings of the women and men of a ruling class. *Clueless* (its title suggesting its central character's lack of insight) centres on the romantic and social machinations of a hierarchical society. At the top, are the patriarchal father figures, providing their daughters with the financial freedom to meddle and such emotional indulgence that they believe they are never wrong. At the bottom are those unfortunates who lack the right look, manner and associations to be accepted into the 'club'.

Clueless takes the classic *Emma* narrative – good-hearted matchmaker, who mismatches others and thus discovers the true meaning of love for herself – and reworks it to reflect the language and zeitgeist of contemporary (rich) America. It does that with great humour and irony, while making a number of serious points about common preoccupations with status, materialism and the pursuit of perfection. The Emma of *Clueless* is Cher, a high-school queen courted for her looks, in with the right crowd, pampered by her father and immune to anything more worrying than who to date, what to wear and where to go. Even though it may appear initially ridiculous to compare the two periods and their heroines, they share the same cosseted, moneyed lifestyle and are both forced to reconsider their values by the end of the narrative.

Key elements are updated in a way that makes us question our cultural priorities. Emma's mother's death becomes Cher's mother's death during cosmetic surgery. Emma's acceptance and mothering (or smothering) of the *ingénue*, Harriet, becomes Cher's 'adoption' of a dungaree-wearing, pot-smoking, exchange student. These contrasts reflect on the superficial preoccupations of their time and on the fact that little has changed in those preoccupations. The comical tone does not detract from the satire. Emma and Cher are both fantasists and the mismatch between reality and aspiration is the source of much of the comedy. Cher, like Emma is the 'voice' of the text. However, Cher's first-person narration and wordy asides make the language of the film a vehicle for much of its wit. When Cher calls another girl a 'Monet' we learn that this means someone who only looks beautiful from a distance. This is only one example of how the text references classic art in a 'postmodern' way. The text is also highly self-referential. The characters talk about shops, commercials, films, brands, magazines and clothes. Their 'lingo' of snappy insults comment on what is considered socially acceptable and unacceptable – a quality shared by the novel. For example:

> Cher: Shopping with Doctor Seuss again today?
> Dionne: Well, at least I wouldn't skin a collie for my backpack!
> Cher: It's *faux*!

The superficiality that rules Emma's world also rules Cher's. Each text takes delight in the rituals and materialism of its time. Cher introduces her new friend, Tai, to the ins and outs of high schools, quickly dismissing all groups except her own. When Cher gives Tai and her spinster teacher, Mrs Geist, makeovers, she is peacock-proud of her achievements only to see them undermined because she misjudged them. Her rejection of a boorish jock and encounters with a 'gay' would-be boyfriend, and her own desire to retain her chastity, are not statements of principle but rather adornments to her image – something that Austen was always keen to mock in her novels.

Teaching suggestions

Tips

- Make sure students read the original texts first, focusing on character and language. They can then assess how they have been amended and updated. This can help to develop an appreciation of the original novel as well as the extra dimension that films can bring to these classic stories.
- Narrative perspective or 'voice' is difficult to represent visually on film. Encourage your students to think about the strategies the filmmakers adopt to overcome or compensate for this difficulty.
- Discourage students from making value judgments or discriminating between the literary original and the film adaptation. A film requires as much active engagement as a book in terms of questioning its construction, and understanding its themes, messages and content. **Worksheet 39** has details of sequences from the films.

Activities and discussions for students

- Compare Emma and Cher. How do they reflect the period in which they live and to what extent are they representative of a universal type?
- How do the filmmakers evoke a sense of time and place through setting and landscape? See **Worksheet 40**.
- Each of the original novels is promoting a message or set of values. Are the same messages conveyed by the films?
- Numerous film adaptations are based on stories from the Bible. Look at some examples (or other films that portray characters from other religions) and discuss how they adapt the source material. Discuss: Should Hollywood adapt religious texts?
- Some adaptations are based on novels with a first-person perspective, in the form of a diary. Make a film of 'a day in the life of' someone in your community or town. Add their voice-over commentary.
- Hollywood wants to adapt your class for a film. Discuss who you think should play you, your friends and maybe your teacher.
- Choose a short story and plan how you would adapt it. What would you leave out? What would you emphasise? See **Worksheet 41**.
- Choose one word and dramatise it. See how different groups 'adapt' this word in their drama recreations.
- Many towns or counties in the UK are the location of a famous book. Research or visit these places and see how they are portrayed on page and screen.
- The Story of Me: Make an autobiographical or biographical film. See **Worksheet 42**.

Key books

Deborah Cartmell, Imelda Whelehan *Adaptions: From Text to Screen, Screen to Text*, Pluto Press, 2000

Robert Giddings, Erica Sheen (eds) *From Page to Screen: Adaptations of the Classic Novel*, Manchester University Press, 1999

Robert Stam, Alessandra Raengo (eds) *Literature and Film: A Guide to the Theory and Practice of Film Adaptation*, Blackwell, 2004

Websites

<www.pbs.org/wgbh/masterpiece/learningresources/index.html> as part of its public service remit, PBS provides online teachers' guides (and downloadable clips of many literary classics, including Shakespeare, Dickens and the Russian greats).

<www.writingstudio.co.za/page62.html> an excellent and accessible short article on the challenge to a screenwriter of adapting for the screen.

<www.writing-world.com/screen/adaptation.shtml> another brief but highly instructive insight into the difficulties of adapting for the screen.

<www.screenonline.org.uk> probably the UK's definitive film portal and an excellent place to seek out insights into the creation of literary adaptations.

8 | Animated business: Feature films

The complexities of producing a successful animated film in the modern film industry.

Links to GCSE

- Animation is probably the genre that students feel most comfortable with as they will have a lot of experience of it. In Media Studies, the practical activity of animation is emphasised rather than a theoretical or analytical engagement. To support both analysis and production <www.animate.org/>, sponsored by the Arts Council and Channel 4, is an excellent resource. It has exemplar material from amateur animators and links to local animators and animation events. It will help to encourage students to attempt their own animation and gain an understanding of the required skills, commitment and patience.

- Animators are often keen to share their insights and arranging for them to visit can be the best way to introduce students to the practicalities and tricks of animation.

- For a more theoretical perspective, <www.arts.ac.uk/library/4781.htm> is the London University of Arts gateway for digital creation. Although it is advanced for GCSE students, it provides direct insights into what is current and meaningful in the world of animation, especially with its examples of cel and 3D animation.

- In the GCSE English specifications, there is still a reluctance to view animated texts as worthy of study. However, Channel 4 has created an excellent series of animated English classics, such as *Sir Gawain and the Green Knight* (*The English Programme – Film Focus: Animation*). The BBC's *Animated Tales* series is another source of animated texts relevant to the English syllabi. They have also produced the excellent *Animation Nation* (first screened October 2005). This comprehensive documentary about British animation is a conclusive argument for the importance and legitimacy of the form.

User name: **filmgcse@bfi.org.uk**   Password: **gc1603fi**

Focus films

Beauty and the Beast (Gary Trousdale and Kirk Wise, US, 1991)
The Animatrix (Peter Chung and Andy Jones, US/Japan, 2003)
The Incredibles (Brad Bird, US, 2005)

The persistence of vision (the trick of perception that makes ordered and swift static images appear to move if seen in quick succession) is the quirk of illusion that makes animation (and the art of cinema itself) possible. Animation is therefore a mode and a technique, as well as a genre. The foundation of animation is drawing and figurative design, and involves the creation of individual images, often of great artistry. Animation's influences and precursors include primitive cave painting, Greek ceramics and mosaics, religious illuminated manuscripts, Japanese calligraphy and the work of great artists from the Renaissance to modern times.

However, a driving force behind animation is the desire to entertain, amuse and surprise an audience, by making unreal static images seem somehow alive and real. Thus, the proper antecedents of the animated film are satirical cartoons in illustrated magazines, and the cartoon strips in newspapers. These early forms created miniature dramas, comedies and tragedies. Early animation translated these forms to a new mass medium: film. While it began as adult novelty entertainment, animation developed a reputation as a children's genre, particularly with the domination of Disney. Nevertheless, there has been always a niche for different animations, and for many animators there remains the thrill of making the surreal, dreamlike or nightmarish, the magical or monstrous *move*, generating joy and fear in audiences of all ages.

Background

In the beginning, animated shorts were appended to live-action, full-length features as two-dimensional, silent appetisers to amuse the audience before the main picture. They often reflected the behaviour of their actor counterparts (especially Chaplin and Keaton) through anthropomorphic escapades. The advent of Walt Disney's cel animations in the 1920s and the creation of Mickey Mouse represented a sea change not only within the genre, but within the film industry itself. With the addition of synchronised sound, *Steamboat Willie* (Walt Disney and Ub Iwerks, US, 1928) showed that cel animation could be commercially and artistically successful. Disney went on to appropriate, dominate and define the genre.

Other cartoon characters followed in the 1930s and 40s and the rise of the comic (*Superman* especially) supplied source material for the new genre. A significant development of this period was the inclination to produce animated versions of live-action features. *Mr. Bug Goes To Town* (Dave Fleischer, US, 1941) is an abbreviated version of the Capra classic, *Mr. Deeds Goes to Town* (Frank Capra, US 1936). The highly popular Mickey Mouse character was used to produce propaganda-style cartoons during the war, and the Disney series, *Silly Symphonies*, garnered Academy Awards. These developments showed a genre growing in maturity and precocity, ready to challenge the status quo of cartoons as the supporting feature. The first full-length animation feature produced by Walt Disney in the US was *Snow White and the Seven Dwarfs* (1937). Considering the time-consuming nature of creating animation, the sophisticated narrative and imagery of *Snow White* represented a peak of commercial and artistic endeavour. Disney's success lay in its improvement of the depth of field in animations and the creation of a production-line system to drawing, inking and setting. The film established many of the genre's conventions – supernatural, mythic or fairytale narratives, human-like movements, intense colouration and songs. Animation was becoming more three-dimensional in every sense of the word.

The 1940s (considered a golden age in the genre) witnessed animation's assault on mainstream cinema. *Pinocchio* (Hamilton Luske and Ben Sharpsteen, US, 1940) with its multiplane technique to create a greater sense of depth, and the attempt at high-culture gravitas with *Fantasia* (James Alger et al, US, 1940) again demonstrated innovation; and the desire to stretch generic boundaries has always motivated the development of the field. Warner Bros. and MGM produced key character-based cartoon series like *Bugs Bunny* and *Tom and Jerry* during this productive era.

In the 1950s and 60s many Disney apprentices moved to other studios to explore their own themes and concerns. New technical advances in the form of pixilation, stop-motion animation and the inclusion of animation in live-action features (exemplified by *Tom Thumb* (George Pal, US, 1958) and *Mary Poppins* (Robert Stevenson, US, 1964)) gained animation critical as well as popular accolades. Animated adaptations of literary works, such as *Animal Farm* (John Halas, UK, 1954), *Charlottes Web* (Charles A. Nichols and Iwao Takamoto, US, 1973), *Watership Down* (Martin Rosen, UK, 1978), and *The Lord of the Rings* (Ralph Bakshi, UK, 1978) saw the genre tackling more serious source material, increasing its versatility while accommodating much darker, domestic, epic or allegorical meanings.

In the 1970s and 80s animation continued to change and develop with the advent of a rival production line by Don Bluth, the fusion of computer-generated technology and animation in *Star Wars* (George Lucas, US, 1977) and Disney's *Tron* (Steven Lisberger, US, 1982). Disney was reinvigorated with the success of *Beauty and the Beast*. At the same time claymation became popular, exemplified in the UK by the award-winning *Wallace and Gromit* (Nick Park, 1995–2005) TV series and films.

The 1990s witnessed a creative explosion in CGI animation, while animators also sought fresh inspiration in Japanese manga and anime, typified by *Ghost in the Shell* (Mamoro Oshii, Japan, 1995) and *Spirited Away* (Hayao Miyazaki, Japan, 2001). With films such as *Toy Story* (John Lasseter, US, 1995), *Monsters Inc.* (Peter Docter, US, 2001), *The Incredibles* (Brad Bird, US, 2004), and the *Shrek* franchise (US, 2000–7), animation has become well-established as a form that appeals to mass audiences and critics alike. At the same time, live-action films for adult-only audiences are beginning to adopt the conventions of animation, as represented, for example, by *Waking Life* (Richard Linklater, US, 2001), *Sin City* (Frank Miller, US, 2005) and *A Scanner Darkly* (Richard Linklater, US, 2005).

Beauty and the Beast

Fairytales have proved a reliable source material for animation. This persistence of magic and mystery has recently been mocked by Pixar's *Shrek* franchise in order to differentiate itself from the 'Disneyfied' competition. However, Pixar's irreverence, even though it reflects a new creative confidence, cannot disguise animation's reliance on ancient tales.

Beauty and the Beast

The *Beauty and the Beast* narrative is antique in it origins; many traditions and societies have attempted to claim it. The story is a meta-narrative like *Cinderella* or *Sleeping Beauty* that appears in some form in most cultures. These meta-narratives can be recognised in many texts: for example *Pretty Woman* = *Cinderella*; *King Kong* (Merian C Cooper, US, 1933) = *Beauty and the Beast*. An early written version of *Beauty and the Beast* was published in 18th-century France. The most memorable and significant film version prior to Disney's *Beauty and the Beast* was Jean Cocteau's 1946 Gothic version *La Belle et La Bête* (France).

Beauty and the Beast is an ideal Disney vehicle because its message of 'beauty within' chimes with the corporation's ideology of inclusiveness. The original story is presented in a visual form and abridged to increase its entertainment value. The animation is grounded in a solid narrative and delivers an exciting visual spectacle, as demonstrated in the film's key scenes (especially the computer-enhanced ballroom scene). The film can revel in its ability to animate and fill with life that which is inanimate. This 'anthropomorphic' approach, where teapots sing and dishes dance, is highly effective as entertainment.

In modernising, updating and refreshing traditional texts, animation interprets them visually for new generations. They can be criticised for being flippant and lacking substance and accused of cashing in (Disney's *Beauty and the Beast* is a big franchise) but this is not a new phenomenon: these tales have been reworked and reinterpreted repeatedly by storytellers who have exploited the basic (almost primeval) appeal of these meta-narratives.

However much these ancient tales are rendered contemporary, they adhere to traditional views of gender and social hierarchy. *Beauty and the Beast* reflects traditional notions about romantic love and male domination. Perhaps this reflects traditions within the animation industry. The early innovators of the genre were men and the industry is still controlled by a coterie of male animators, with few female writers or directors breaking through.

The Animatrix

The rise of manga and anime represents the most serious recent challenge to mainstream Western animation. The market for manga and anime has grown steadily from its Asian-Pacific roots to infiltrate Western youth culture. Its sophisticated storytelling and kinetic imagery have begun to influence texts as diverse as *The Lion King* (Roger Allers, US, 1994) and *The Simpsons* series. However, Western industry has a tendency to

The Animatrix

appropriate and adapt 'alternative' work to make it palatable for a mainstream audience. Thus anime and manga still tend to be seen 'outside', 'Eastern' genres, that can be referenced but are rarely actively promoted. However, it is simplistic to suggest that Hollywood 'steals' ideas and styles from Japan. Closer to the truth is that there is mutual exploitation, with each industry influencing and inspiring the other and many leading animators working in both camps.

Manga and anime are distinct genres. Manga are comic books that inspire their animated versions – anime. The significant difference between Western and Eastern styles is that anime is cross-genre, cross-gender, and cross-age. Japanese animation has a breadth of speciality, meaning all tastes are catered for – however deviant and extreme those tastes may be. The film *The Animatrix* (Peter Chung and Andy Jones, US/Japan, 2003) is a compilation of nine short animations, commissioned by the Wachowski brothers to bridge the story between *The Matrix* and *The Matrix Reloaded*. Primarily, *The Animatrix* is a homage to and acknowledgment of anime's influence on the *Matrix* films. The cartoonish action, sexualised style, suggestion of alternate universes and techno-chic are qualities associated with anime. *The Animatrix* is also a convenient and low-budget method for filling in the back story of *The Matrix Reloaded* and whetting the appetite of the viewer. *The Animatrix* is a way for the directors to retain their audience while reaching out to new fans and viewers. There is a growing trend to commission animated versions of successful films. This reversal, where films are now the source material for animation, is evidence for the rising economic power of animation films.

The Animatrix is a mainstream vehicle for an alternative art form. Classic manga and anime have always had a specialist edge and only now are they making a breakthrough into the wider commercial market outside the Asian arena. Acclaimed texts such as *Akira* (Otomo Katsuhiro, Japan, 1988), *Ghost in the Shell* and *Spirited Away* show that anime is able to turn its culturally specific origins into universal themes and dramas. The global rise of animeted children's television series and their film versions, such as *Pokémon*: *The Movie* (Kunihiko Yuyuma, Japan/US, 1999), and *Dragonball Z 2* (Shigeyasu Yamauchi, Japan, 1996), reveal the growing appetite of a key youth market for manga and anime.

This ability to appeal to both a pliant youth market and an older market (who may have purchased manga in their youth) with disposable income, has become a significant motivator in the creation of new animated films. The crossover films, bridging the adult and child audience, unite the most profitable of demographics. Many of these narratives contain physical comedy and spectacle to entertain the younger audience members while the intertextuality and 'knowingness' of much of the dialogue and pop-culture references satisfy the more mature members.

The Incredibles

It is rare to find a film, unless it emerges from the independent sector, that is not sustained by an extensive multimedia campaign. Films are traditionally supported by commercials, posters, adverts and trailers – all attempting to generate that crucial 'word-of-mouth' response in the target audience. However, as animation reaches new heights of artistic endeavour, there is a

The Incredibles

growing sense that sometimes the text is secondary to the marketing and merchandise aims allied with the original film.

The Incredibles (Brad Bird, US, 2004) has proved to be one of the most commercially successful of recent animated films. The film's sophisticated animation and story about retired superheroes and family dysfunction, plays well to a wide audience. However, there are other aspect to its success. Even though modern animated films still begin with drawn characters and an outline narrative, other branches of the business quickly make their presence and needs apparent. The development of a film and its promotion takes several years and involves many strategies. The animation business, with its instant avenue to young purchasers who grow into older purchasers with more disposable income, is always eager to find new outlets. One marketing strategy is to trail and preview new films in recently successful ones; for example, there are references to *The Incredibles* in *Finding Nemo* (Andrew Stanton, US, 2003). Another one is to continue the successful films with sequels or franchises. While in the past most popular animations were followed by sequels that went straight to video, now such films as *Toy Story 2* (John Lasseter, US, 1999), or *Shrek 2* (Andrew Adamson, US, 2004) and *Shrek the Third* (Chris Miller, US, 2007) illustrate the expansion of the animated franchise.

Other ways of promoting the films include extensive merchandising such as toys, computer games, and food branding. Films like *The Incredibles* have spawned comic versions, novelisations, board games and animated series, demonstrating the growing power of animation to set the creative and financial agenda. For example, the lucrative *Star Wars* franchise is now committed to extending its universe in an animated series, well after the release of the final instalment.

Teaching suggestions

Tips

- For Media Studies GCSE, the BFI teaching pack *Into Animation* (<www.bfi.org.uk/education/teaching/intoanimation>) contains useful short animations and extracts for focused study – unfortunately it is only available on VHS. BFI Screenonline (<www.screenonlineorg.uk>) features a lot of great animation material and will help to encourage students to view animation as an adult genre and to question it critically.
- For English GCSE syllabi, animated adaptations of classic texts can make a useful focus. **Worksheet 43** has details of sequences from the films.

Activities and discussions for students

- Look at the Beast and Pierre in *Beauty and the Beast*. How do they compare as ideas of what it is to be a man?
- Female roles are usually well defined in animation. What kind of 'roles' do women play and how do these fit with expectations?
- *The Animatrix* showcases different types of animation. Which is the most effective and why?

- Look at *Fantasia*, a bold attempt by Disney to turn animation into a more respected, creative art form. Do you think it succeeded?
- Research the development of animation. Use **Worksheet 44** (also applicable to other genres).
- Why do filmmakers use special effects sequences? See **Worksheet 45**. It can be used for other genres.
- Discuss: Who is animation really for – children or adults?
- Animated films rely heavily on fairytales. Watch the animated version of a fairytale and then write an updated version of the story for a 21st-century audience.
- Animate your friends. Tell a story by arranging your friends in a series of freeze frames in silence. Invite other students to guess the story. Add 'speech bubbles'. The same task can be done on video. Film your arranged figures. Freeze frame them. Swap work with another group and add captions.
- Most art colleges now offer degree courses in animation. Encourage students to go to see the work that young animators are producing.

Key books

James Clarke *Animated Films*, Virgin Books, 2004
Jonathan Clements, Helen McCarthy *The Anime Encyclopaedia: A Guide to Japanese Animation Since 1917*, Stone Bridge Press, 2001
Paul Wells *Understanding Animation*, Routledge, 2002
Julius Wiedemann *Animation Now!* Taschen, 2004

Websites

an excellent site looking at the heyday of Hollywood mainstream animation.
<www.animationnation.com> In-depth academic essays on the practice and industry of animation.
<www.bcdb.com/bcdb/page.cgi?d=1%001> a massive catalogue of online classic cartoons and a significant database of new animation.

Glossary

180° rule
An imaginary axis which governs where cameras can be placed in order to maintain the illusion of continuity when filming a sequence. By not 'crossing' the imaginary line, characters within a scene maintain the right left/right position. Deviating from it can make figures and actions seem wrong and lack narrative coherence.

Action
Everything that takes place within the frame of the text and a word that often signifies the kinetic movement of actors and the circumstances they are involved in.

Adaptation
A term that is used to describe the translation of material from one genre to another – this process is not always one way (fiction to film).

Alternative
Within a film context, this is a term attributed to films that seem to challenge the status quo in style, themes or content. These texts often exist outside the mainstream and conventional modes of creation or distribution.

Animation
The rapid display of a sequence of images of 2-D artwork, 3D, or models in order to create an illusion of movement. It is an optical illusion of motion due to the phenomenon of persistence of vision.

Animatronics
Robots and electronics puppets that are often used for special effects in films, for example sea creatures, giant monsters etc.

Antagonist
In conventional narrative, the character who stands in opposition to the values or goals of the protagonist. The actions of the antagonist may precipitate the journey of the protagonist or may impede his or her narrative progression. Generally, audiences are positioned so that they have little empathy with the antagonists.

Auteur
A term derived from French film criticism, suggesting that the director is the sole author of any text and the guiding force of creation.

Blockbuster
A term that describes highly financially successful films, mostly big-budget event movies that often dominate the busy summer release schedule.

Bluescreen
The filmmaking technique of using a blue background (in front of which characters or objects are placed) for the purpose of replacing it with a different image or scene. The term also refers to the visual effect resulting from this technique as well as the colored screen itself (although it is often not blue: for example, with greenscreen).

Glossary

Box office

Box-office business can be measured in terms of the number of people who see a film or the amount of money raised by ticket sales. The projection and analysis of these earnings is very important for the creative industries and often a source of interest for fans.

Budget

The money available to filmmakers to finance all the constituent elements of filmmaking (cast, sets, locations etc).

CGI

Stands for computer-generated imagery mostly used to create visual or special effects; a foundation stone of modern cinema but once the most avant-garde special effect. Essentially, computer graphics become a composite part of a film scene.

Closure

The moment of resolution, usually at the end of a (film) text. Most mainstream films ensure that all narrative strands are successfully ended. More alternative texts often have open endings in which there is little attempt to resolve narrative issues or questions.

Connotation

Complements denotation (a basic description of a text's elements). Examining a text at a connotative level means discovering its multiple meanings, values and associations.

Continuity editing

The editing style characteristic of the Hollywood system and classic narratives for the showing of cause and effect.

Cultural imperialism

A term that describes one nation asserting its social values, codes and priorities through its filmic art. For critics it can be both an implicit and explicit agenda. Some countries hope to protect themselves from cultural imperialism by restricting the exhibition of foreign films (eg France places restrictions on the exhibition of US films).

Deep focus

Related to the positioning of objects within the film frame and their depth of field. This technique was an advance on previous methods as it allowed all elements within the frame to be held in sharp focus. The opposite is shallow focus.

Demographic

A term that assists in identifying and segmenting a target audience and then marketing specifically to that group. Creators of film texts may make a film with a key demographic appeal in mind – eg 18–25-year-old males. Some film genres are associated with certain demographics. Typical categories are age, race, class and gender.

Diegetic sound

Any sound presented as originated from source within the film's world. Sound whose source is visible on the screen or whose source is implied to be present by the action of the film.

Fandom

A network or 'collective' of fans who are dedicated to following and understanding certain film texts. They may develop their devotion into a wider culture, for example there are *Star Wars* fans who advocate the 'Jedi' faith.

Franchise

A term that describes a highly successful series of films that may be revisited or reinterpreted by new generations of filmmakers for often greater commercial gain.

Gender

The cultural formulation of biological difference. Masculinity and femininity refer to qualities that are culturally ascribed to male and female behaviour. These qualities may change over time and are open to debate and challenge in ways that biological definitions are not.

Genre

More than the type or category of film, this term also describes the recognisable features, conventions and patterns of a text or a collection of texts.

Hegemony

The process through which dominant ideologies establish themselves as uncontested values. A text could be described as 'hegemonic' if it does not attempt to challenge values that are considered to be 'normal'. Linked to cultural imperialism.

High-key lighting

Opposed to low-key lighting, this is lighting that creates an even look with minimal contrast.

Homage

A text or textual element that pays tribute to another text by following its conventions or style.

Hybrid

A term that describes a film that may be an amalgam or mixture of other influences and texts. It often describes the merging of distinct genres – eg comedy horror films.

Iconography

The study of images such as those images that have an important significance to a particular culture or time. Discussing imagery as iconography in this way implies a critical 'reading' of imagery that often attempts to explore social and cultural values.

Ideology

A complex term. Basically one that describes the natural assumptions, beliefs and values of a film text.

Intertextuality

The borrowing or 'reflection' of elements from another text to create new or familiar meanings. It is linked to homage – some critics have called it the film equivalent of stealing from another film without getting caught.

Juxtaposition

Placing one thing next to another – can occur within a frame (cinematography) or in time (editing).

Low culture

A pejorative term that suggests a text is unworthy of study or without artistic merit. Early cinema was considered 'low culture' as it was seemingly disposable. Although cinema is established as an art form – some genres within the form are still considered 'low', such as gross-out comedy.

Low-key lighting

Illumination with heavy contrast between light and dark; used mostly for noir and horror films.

Mainstream

Something that is mainstream is considered to have the widest appeal to the majority of people.

Glossary

Melodrama

A genre within itself but also a term that describes a text that is extreme in its emotional elements and is therefore expected to elicit extreme emotions from the audience.

Merchandising

The manner in which a text is promoted and marketed. It can also refer to products that often accompany a film release (clothing, toys, posters etc).

Mise en scène

From the French, meaning literally 'put into the scene'. Includes such aspects as location, set, props, costume, make up and lighting.

Narrative

The events happening to characters within a story and told over time, in chronological order.

Non-diegetic sound

Sound not produced by a source within the world of the story; for example, a voice-over or music.

Parody

A text that mocks and ridicules the conventions or elements of another text. Sometimes known as a spoof, it is often created for comedic effect.

Polysemy

A phrase that describes the way a text or a textual element has the potential to carry multiple meanings.

Protagonist

A term that describes the hero or central character of a film. They typically lead the action and the film focuses on their emotional journey.

Representation

The ability of texts to draw upon features of the world and present them to the viewer as constructions, presenting 'versions of reality' influenced by culture and peoples. Representations are, as a result, influenced by culture and, in much the same way, have the capacity to shape culture and mould society's attitudes, values, perceptions and behaviours.

Semiology

The study of signs and symbols, and the creation of meaning in a text. One of the tools for the study of films.

Sequel

A follow-up to an often successful, original film. Most film contracts have a commitment to a sequel written in. A sequel has all the recognisable elements of the first film but tries to extend and develop the characters and narrative.

Shallow focus

The opposite of deep focus, in which only a limited number of elements within the frame (usually those in the foreground) can be clearly seen.

Star

The 'star' is the main actor in a film and their presence can dictate a film's success. Some stars are allied to certain film genres. The term suggests the removed nature and elevated status of film celebrities.

Stereotype

Stereotyping is a process in which a group is simplified into basic characteristics. This is often because stereotypes are highly recognisable and act as instant shorthand to a target audience. In extremes, they can be considered racist and sexist and therefore undesirable.

Subvert

To subvert means to undermine and challenge expectations.

Target audiences

Linked to market research and the method of finding an audience – audiences are targeted in terms of age, gender, social status.

Textual analysis

The main method for the study of the meaning of a text; for decoding it.

Theme

The grand idea that underlies a film text, essentially the message that the audience takes from the text as a whole, either as part of its genre (Western – revenge, romantic comedy – love) or as a result of the film's agenda.

Zeitgeist

The spirit of an age/of it's time, denoting the cultural and intellectual climate of an era. Increasingly film texts are creating wider social meanings, embodying a zeitgeist by reflecting their era through their images and intentions.

Filmography

$8\frac{1}{2}$ (Federico Fellini, Italy, 1963)
10 Things I Hate About You (Gil Junger, US, 1999)
About a Boy (Paul Weitz, Germany/US/France/UK, 2002)
About a Girl (Brian Percival, UK, 2001)
The Adventures of Prince Achmed (Lotte Reiniger, Germany, 1926)
Akira (Otomo Katsuhiro, Japan, 1988)
Adaptation (Spike Jonze, US, 2002)
Alfie (Gilbert Lewis, UK, 1966)
Amélie (Jean-Pierre Jeunet, France, 2001)
American History X (Tony Kaye, US, 1998)
American Pie (US, 1999–2003) trilogy
Animal Farm (John Halas, UK, 1954)
The Animatrix (Peter Chung and Andy Jones, US/Japan, 2003)
Apocalypse Now (Francis Coppola, US, 1979)
Armageddon (Michael Bay, US, 1998)
Back to the Future (Robert Zemeckis, US, 1985)
Batman (Lambert Hillier, US, 1943)
Batman (Tim Burton, US, 1989)
Batman Begins (Christopher Nolan, UK/US, 2005)
Batman Forever (Joel Schumacher, US, 1995)
Batman Returns (Tim Burton, US, 1992)
Batman & Robin (Joel Schumacher, US, 1997)
The Battleship Potemkin (Sergei Eisenstein, USSR, 1925)
Beauty and the Beast (Gary Trousdale and Kirk Wise, US, 1991)
La Belle et La Bête (Jean Cocteau, France, 1946)
Bend It Like Beckham (Gurinder Chadha, UK, 2002)
Ben-Hur (William Wyler, UK, 1959)
Billy Elliot (Stephen Daldry, UK, 2000)
The Blackboard Jungle (Richard Brooks, US, 1955)
Bladerunner (Ridley Scott, US, 1982)
Boyz N The Hood (John Singleton, US, 1991)
Brazil (Terry Gilliam, UK, 1984)
Bride and Prejudice (Gurinder Chada, UK/Germany, 2004)
Bridget Jones franchise (2001–4)
Brighton Rock (John Boulting, UK, 1947)
Brother (Kitano Takeshi, Japan/UK/USA, 2003)
Bullet Boy (Saul Dibb, UK, 2004)
The Cabinet of Dr Caligari (Robert Wiene, Germany, 1920)

Casablanca (Michael Curtiz, US, 1942)

Charlottes Web (Charles A. Nichols and Iwao Takamoto, US,1973)

Un Chien Andalou (Luis Buñuel & Salvador Dali, France, 1929)

A Christmas Carol (Edwin L Marin, US, 1938)

A Christmas Carol (Clive Donner, US, 1984)

A Christmas Carol (David Hugh Jones, US, 1999)

Clueless (Amy Heckerling, US, 1995)

Con Air (Simon West, US, 1997)

Dark City (Alex Proyas, US/Australia, 1998)

Dark Water (Hideo Nakata, Japan, 2002)

The Day after Tomorrow (Roland Emmerich, US, 2004)

Die Hard franchise (US, 1988–2007)

Dirty Dancing (Emile Ardolino, US, 1987)

Donnie Darko (Richard Kelly, US, 2001)

Dragonball Z 2 (Shigeyasu Yamauchi, Japan, 1996)

Early Summer (Yasujiro Ozu, Japan, 1951)

Elephant (Gus van Sant, US, 2003)

The End of the Affair (Neil Jordan, Germany/US, 1999)

Equinox Flower (Yasujiro Ozu, Japan, 1958),

The Faculty (Michel Mann, US, 1999)

Fantasia (James Alger et al, US, 1940)

Fever Pitch (David Evans, UK, 1996)

Finding Nemo (Andrew Stanton, US, 2003)

Footloose (Herbert Ross, US, 1984)

Four Weddings and a Funeral (Mike Newell, UK, 1994)

The Full Monty (Peter Cattaneo, UK, 1997)

Ghost in the Shell (Mamoro Oshii, Japan, 1995)

The Gladiator (Edward Sedgewick, US, 1938)

Godzilla (Roland Emmerich, US, 1998)

GoldenEye (Martin Campbell, UK/US, 1995)

The Goonies (Richard Donner, US, 1985)

Gremlins (Joe Dante, US, 1984)

Hamlet (Franco Zeffirelli, US/France, 1990)

Harry Potter franchise (2001–present)

Henry V (Laurence Olivier, UK, 1944)

High Fidelity (Stephen Frears, US/UK, 2000)

Howard's End (James Ivory, Japan/UK, 1992)

The Hulk (Ang Lee, US, 2003)

An Inconvenient Truth (Davis Guggenheim, US, 2006)

The Incredibles (Brad Bird, US, 2004)

Independence Day (Roland Emmerich, US, 1996)

Indiana Jones franchise (US, 1981–2008)

It Happened One Night (Frank Capra, US, 1934)

It's a Boy Girl Thing (Nick Hurran, UK/Canada, 2006)

Jaws (Steven Spielberg, US, 1975)

The Jazz Singer (Alan Crossland, US, 1927)

Julius Caesar (Joseph L Mankiewicz, US, 1953)

Kids (Larry Clark, US, 1995)

The King and I (Walter Lang, US, 1956)

King Kong (Merian C Cooper, US, 1933)

Labyrinth (Jim Henson, US, 1986)

The Lady in the Lake (Robert Montgomery, US, 1947)

The Last Samurai (Edward Zwick, US, 2003)

Late Spring (Ozu Yasujiro, Japan, 1949)

The Lavender Hill Mob (Charles Crichton, UK, 1951)

Lethal Weapon 3 (Richard Donner, US, 1992)

The Lion King (Roger Allers, US, 1994)

The Lord of the Rings (Ralph Bakshi, UK, 1978)

The Lord of the Rings trilogy (Peter Jackson, US/NZ, 2001–3)

The Lord of the Rings: The Fellowship of the Ring (Peter Jackson, US/NZ, 2001)

Lost in La Mancha (Keith Fulton and Luis Pepe, UK/US, 2002)

Love Actually (Richard Curtis, UK, 2004)

Macbeth (Roman Polanski, US, 1948)

Macbeth (Orson Welles, US, 1948)

The Man with the Golden Arm (Otto Preminger, US, 1955)

Mary Poppins (Robert Stevenson, US, 1964)

The Matrix (Andy and Larry Wachowski, US/Australia, 1999)

The Matrix Reloaded (Andy and Larry Wachowski, US, 2003)

The Matrix Revolutions (Andy and Larry Wachowski, US, 2003)

Maytime in Mayfair (Herbert Wilcox, UK, 1949)

Mean Girls (Mark S Waters, US, 2004)

Memento (Christopher Nolan, US, 2000)

Metropolis (Fritz Lang, Germany, 1927).

A Midsummer Night's Dream (Michael Hoffmann, US/Germany, 1999)

Mr. Bug Goes To Town (Dave Fleischer, US, 1941)

Mr. Deeds Goes to Town (Frank Capra, US 1936)

Monsters Inc. (Peter Docter, US, 2001)

The Most Beautiful Man in the World (Alicia Duffy, UK, 2002)

Napoleon Dynamite (Jared Hess, US, 2004)

A Nightmare on Elm Street (Wes Craven, US, 1984)

Nosferatu (F W Murnau, Germany, 1922)

Notting Hill (Roger Michell, UK, 1999)

O (Tim Blake Nelson, US, 2001)

An Officer and a Gentleman (Taylor Hackford, US, 1982)

A Passage to India (James Ivory, UK/US, 1984)

Passport To Pimlico (Henry Cornelius, UK, 1949)

Pillow Talk (Michael Gordon, US, 1959)

Pinocchio (Hamilton Luske and Ben Sharpsteen, US, 1940)

Pleasantville (Gary Ross, US, 1998)

Pokémon: The Movie (Kunihiko Yuyuma, Japan/US, 1999)

The Power and the Glory (Marc Daniels, US, 1961)

Pretty Woman (Garry Marshall, US, 1992)

Filmography

Princess Monoke (Hayao Miyazaki, Japan, 1997)

Punch Drunk Love (Paul Thomas Anderson, US, 2002)

Psycho, Alfred Hitchcock, US, 1960

The Rainbow (Ken Russell, UK, 1989)

Rashomon (Akira Kurosawa, Japan, 1949)

Rear Window (Alfred Hitchcock, US, 1954)

Rebel Without A Cause (Nicholas Ray, US, 1955)

The Ring (Nakata Hideo, Japan, 1998)

The Rock (Michael Bay, US, 1994)

Rocky (John G Avildsen, US, 1976)

Romeo and Juliet (George Cukor, US, 1936)

Romeo and Juliet (Franco Zeffirelli, UK/Italy, 1968)

Room at the Top (Jack Clayton, UK, 1959)

A Room With A View (James Ivory, UK, 1985)

Saturday Night and Sunday Morning (Karel Reisz, UK, 1960)

A Scanner Darkly (Richard Linklater, US, 2005)

Scarface (Howard Hawks, US, 1933)

Scream (Wes Craven, US, 1996)

Scrooge (Brian Desmond Hurst, UK, 1951)

Scrooge (Ronald Neame, UK, 1970)

Scrooged (Richard Donner, US, 1988)

The Searchers (John Ford, US, 1956)

Seven Samurai (Akira Kurosawa, Japan, 1954)

Shakespeare in Love (John Madden, US, 1998)

Shall We Dance (Masayuki Suo, Japan, 1996)

Shaun of the Dead (Edgar Wright, UK, 2004)

She's the Man (Andy Fickman, US, 2006)

Shrek (Andrew Adamson, US, 2001)

Shrek 2 (Andrew Adamson, US, 2004)

Shrek the Third (Chris Miller, US, 2007)

Sin City (Frank Miller, US, 2005)

Sky Captain and the World of Tomorrow (Kerry Conran, US, 2004)

Snow White and the Seven Dwarfs (Walt Disney, US, 1937)

Sonatine (Kitano Takeshi, Japan, 1993)

Spider-man (Sam Raimi, US, 2002)

Spirited Away (Hayao Miyazaki, Japan, 2002)

Spring in Park Lane (Herbert Wilcox, UK, 1948)

Stand By Me (Rob Reiner, US, 1986)

Star Wars (George Lucas, US, 1977)

Steamboat Willie (Walt Disney and Ub Iwerks, US, 1928)

Strike (Sergei Eisenstein, USSR, 1925)

Superman: The Movie (Richard Donner, US, 1978)

Superman 2 (Richard Lester, US, 1980)

Superman 4 (Sidnie J Furie, US, 1987)

Superman Returns (Bryan Singer, US, 2006)

Swamp Thing (Wes Craven, US, 1982)

Filmography

The Taming of the Shrew (Sam Taylor, US, 1929)

The Terminator (James Cameron, US, 1984)

The Terminator 2: Judgment Day (James Cameron, US, 1991)

The Terminator 3: The Rise of the Machines (Jonathan Mostow, US, 2003)

Thirteenth Floor (Joseph Rusnak, US/Germany, 1999)

*Throne of Blood (*Akira Kurosawa, Japan, 1957)

To Kill a Mockingbird (Robert Mulligan, US, 1962)

Tokyo Drifter (Suzuki Seijun, Japan, 1966)

Tokyo Story (Yasujiro Ozu, Japan, 1953)

Tom Thumb (George Pal, US, 1958)

Top Gun (Tony Scott, US, 1986)

Toy Story (John Lasseter, US, 1995)

Toy Story 2 (John Lasseter, US, 1999)

The Tragedy of Macbeth (Roman Polanski, US/UK, 1971)

The Tragedy of Othello: The Moor of Venice (Orson Welles, US, 1952)

Trainspotting (Danny Boyle, UK, 1996)

Tron (Steven Lisberger, US, 1982)

True Lies (James Cameron, US, 1994)

Twelfth Night (Trevor Nunn, UK, 1999)

The Twilight Samurai (Yoji Yamada, Japan, 2003)

Unbreakable (M Night Shyamalan, US, 2000)

The Urban Savannah (Matthew Cooke, Vincent Lund, UK, 2004)

V for Vendetta (James McTeigue, US/Germany, 2006)

Vertical Limit (Martin Campbell, US, 2000)

A Voyage to the Moon (George Méliès, France, 1902)

Waking Life (Richard Linklater, US, 2001)

Wallace and Gromit films (Nick Park, 1995–2005)

Watership Down (Martin Rosen, UK, 1978)

West Side Story (Robert Wise, US, 1961)

Westworld (Michael Crichton, US, 1973)

When Harry Met Sally (Rob Reiner, US, 1989)

Who's Afraid of Virginia Wolf (Mike Nichols, US, 1966)

The Wild One (Laszlo Benedek, US,1953)

Wild, Wild West (Barry Sonnenfeld, US, 1999)

William Shakespeare's Romeo + Juliet (Baz Luhrmann, US/Canada, 1996)

The Wizard of Oz (Victor Fleming, US, 1939)

Women in Love (Ken Russell, UK, 1969)

Wonder Woman (Vincent McEveety, US, 1974)

X-Men (Bryan Singer, US, 2000)

X-Men 3: The Last Stand (Brett Ratner, US/UK, 2006)

Yojimbo (Akira Kurosawa, Japan, 1961)